Battlegr

MW00982347

OPERATION VARSITY
Rhine Crossing

THE BRITISH & CANADIAN
AIRBORNE ASSAULT

Battleground Europe

OPERATION VARSITY
Rhine Crossing

THE BRITISH & CANADIAN
AIRBORNE ASSAULT

Tim Saunders

Pen & Sword
MILITARY

This book is dedicated to my father Ron Saunders who 'served' as a Sea Scout during these days.

First published in Great Britain in 2008 by
Pen & Sword Military
an imprint of
Pen & Sword Books Ltd
47 Church Street
Barnsley
South Yorkshire
S70 2AS

ISBN 978 1 84415 601 6

A CIP catalogue record for this book is
available from the British Library.

Typeset in Palatino

Printed and bound in the United Kingdom by CPI

Pen & Sword Books Ltd incorporates the imprints of Pen & Sword Aviation, Pen
& Sword Maritime, Pen & Sword Military, Wharncliffe Local History, Pen and
Sword Select, Pen and Sword Military Classics and Leo Cooper.
For a complete list of Pen & Sword titles, please contact
Pen & Sword Books Limited
47 Church Street, Barnsley, South Yorkshire, S70 2AS, England
E-mail: enquiries@pen-and-sword.co.uk
Website: www.pen-and-sword.co.uk

CONTENTS

Introduction

This is the third **Battleground** title on the Rhine Crossing. It covers the airborne aspects of the operation, focusing on the British 6th Airborne Division, but also includes sufficient background to place VARSITY into its correct context alongside the other operations to cross Germany's last strategic barrier. It includes details of XII Corps's assault crossing, as ignoring the troops who were to 'relieve' 6th Airborne in a closely coordinated plan would paint an incomplete picture.

Operation PLUNDER was the overall name for 21st Army Group's crossing of the Rhine but each of the major elements was known by its own codeword – VARSITY the airborne operation, TURNSCREW and TORCHLIGHT the British assault river crossings, WIGEON the attack by 1 Commando Brigade on Wesel and FLASHLIGHT the XVI US Corps crossing.

The airborne plan incorporated virtually every lesson of the disaster that befell 6th Airborne Divisions 'brother division' at Arnhem. Gone were the cavalier assumptions that the war would be over quickly and easily after the Germans' collapse in Normandy. In fact, the enemy was showing every sign of fighting to the bitter end, arguably as a result of the Allied insistence on unconditional surrender. The depth of the liaison between the ground troops and the airborne element was remarkable. Plans, amongst others, were made to ensure that there was a prompt link up and that, in the event of difficulty, there would be communications to facilitate an appropriate and timely response.

As is my practice I have standardized a number of place names with the modern spelling as found on signposts, chief of these is DIESERFORDTERWALD, which had a variety of spellings in both Allied and German documents and maps.

Vorsicht

Panzerfaust
100m

1. Kopf abnehmen.
2. Kopf senkrecht halten u. Zündladung 34 so einsetzen, daß das Papier-Abdeckblatt sichtbar ist.
3. Zünder einsetzen mit dem Zündhütchen gegen das Papier-Abdeckblatt.
4. Kopf wieder aufstecken.
5. Die Pappkappe am Rohrende bleibt beim Abschuß aufgesetzt. ebx 45

Acknowledgements

The individual museums of the regiments who took part in the Rhine Crossing and of course the Airborne Forces Museum have, as usual, provided excellent and generous help. I would particularly like to thank 'Drummie' Cox of my own regiment, the Devon and Dorsets at Exeter, who provided me with material on 12 Airborne Devons that has not seen the light of day. I am also indebted to Stan Jarvis, who has provided me with a wealth of information on the RAF glider pilots, who so distinguished themselves during the battle. I am similarly grateful to the other veterans who talked to me and provided authoritative written accounts of the battle.

I would also like to thank two friends and colleagues from the Guild of Battlefield Guides, who helped in the researching of this book. Firstly, Major Mike Peters of the Army Air Corps, whose corps, has finally been recognised as successors to the Glider Pilot Regiment with the emblazoning of the GPR battle honours on their colours. Bob Hilton, with over twenty year's service in the Parachute Regiment, drew my attention to sources and helped me check information on the airborne aspects of the book. I am most grateful to them both for their assistance.

At home or on the ground enjoy the tour of the Operation VARSITY battlefield.

Tim Saunders
Warminster 2008

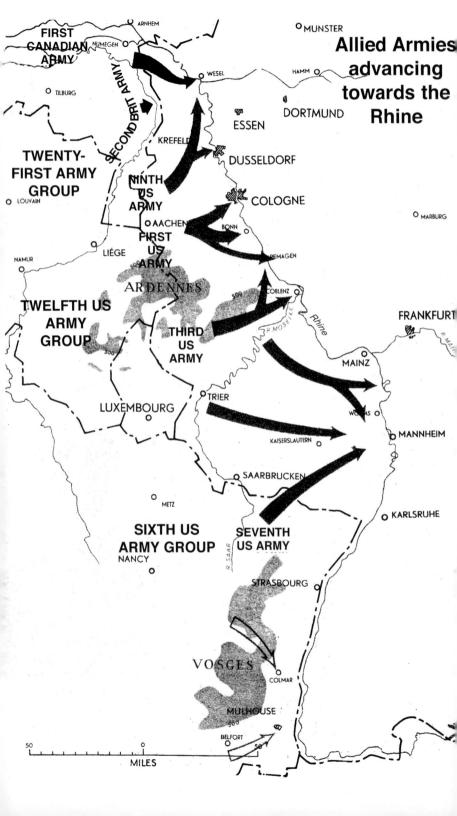

CHAPTER ONE

Background

In early September 1944, 6th Airborne Division returned to its camps on Salisbury Plain, after an almost unique hundred days in contact with the enemy in Normandy. There were many bed spaces left empty or filled by battle casualty replacements, not all of whom had been airborne selected or trained. Meanwhile, the pursuit across northern France frustrated their sister division, 1st Airborne, who despite a succession of nineteen planning cycles, was still kicking its heels at its bases across the east midlands and cruelly being named '1st Stillborn Division' by those looking for a fight. Such was the speed of the ground advance that identified objectives were reached before the airborne operation could be mounted.

The pervading view amongst the Allies was that final victory over Germany was near. So high was the optimism that normally cautious intelligence officers were predicting that victory was 'within sight, almost within reach' and they reported that it was 'unlikely that organized German resistance would continue beyond 1 December 1944'. Dissenting voices who believed that the German forces were not finished and were preparing a 'last-ditch struggle in the field at all costs', were, in the prevailing enthusiasm, ignored.

Obersturmbannführer Hubert Meyer, Chief of Staff of 12th SS Panzer Division *Hitlerjugend*, disputes the claimed completeness of the Allied victory in Normandy.

Your histories claim that my division was reduced to a couple of hundred men.

The last few hundred did have to break out of the Falaise Kessel but they joined almost 12,000 who had already escaped. Although we had lost much equipment, Feldmarschall *Model conducted an excellent withdrawal to the east the significance of which is largely unrecognized.*

***Obersturmbannführer*
Hubert Meyer.**

Consequently, Montgomery in his attempt to 'bounce' 21st Army Group across the Rhine onto the North German Plain in Operation MARKET GARDEN found that the Germans were far from defeated. There was to be no repeat of the 1918 German civil and military collapse that many Great War veteran commanders predicted and no dash into the heart of Germany to finish the war by Christmas 1944. With the Allies stalled, having outrun their supplies, with the weather worsening, 200,000 mostly slave labourers, worked to strengthen the pre-war German defences known as the West Wall or Siegfried Line. The physical barrier was to be manned by new citizen or *volksgrenadier* formations, with Himler calling to arms the young, the old and many men previously excluded from the *Wehrmacht* on grounds of economic necessity, health, etc. To these men, were added the now largely redundant manpower from the *Luftwaffe* and *Kriegsmarine*, who with the *Volksgrenadier* divisions now prepared the defence of the borders of the Third Reich. The Allies had underestimated the German's genius for highly effective military improvisation and were largely unaware of the remarkable strategic recovery the enemy was staging.

With the failure of MARKET GARDEN at Arnhem, General Eisenhower reverted to his broad front strategy. This favoured US doctrine of the time, was politically acceptable in that it would see all three allied army groups fighting on the German frontier, breaching the West Wall and then battling their way to the Rhine; Germany's last strategic barrier. Destruction of the German field armies and the capture of the Ruhr, Germany's industrial powerhouse, were to be the principal objectives rather than a headlong advance across the North German Plain to Berlin. The consequences of this policy were fully apparent to the British, who had an eye on the post-war situation in Europe rather than the simple defeate of Germany.

In the deteriorating autumn weather, which heralded a bad winter, the fighting was costly and Allied progress slowed almost to a halt. Nowhere was progress slower and more expensive in both British and American lives than at the Dutch town of Overloon in the Mass Pocket. Further to the north, the Canadians fought to open the Scheldt Estuary to gain access for shipping to the vital port of Antwerp, which was to be the supply base for the Allied advance into Hitler's Reich. Elsewhere, desperate battles were fought by British and American troops to reach and then penetrate the West Wall, at points such as Geilenkeirchen, where the British 43rd Wessex Division fought alongside the US 84th Division to overcome a determined enemy in weather and ground conditions that foreshadowed those they were to experience later in the winter. Meanwhile, General Patton grumbled and swore, as his armour bogged down in the mud of Lorraine. The Germans fought with courage and determination to defend the borders of their Fatherland and it was obvious that despite the continuing bomber offensive, the war was not going to be won until well into 1945.

The Battle of the Bulge

Hitler's counter-attack with his rebuilt army in the Ardennes in mid-December 1944, launched under the cover of bad weather, caught the Allies by surprise. The German aim was to separate the Allied armies by striking north-west to Antwerp, enveloping and destroying the Ninth US Army, along with the British and Canadian Armies. Initially, the Germans, benefiting from a lax American stance on a lightly held, quiet front, were successful and created a significant 'Bulge' in the Allied lines. However, the relatively inexperienced staffs of the Allied Armies of D Day were now honed to a high state of competence and reacted quickly to close off the German advance before they reached the River Meuse.

Men of 6th Airborne Division, complete with snow suits in the wintry Ardennes.

An airborne section goes to ground as they come under effective enemy fire.

6th Airborne Division were dragged away from what promised to be a grey and frugal Christmas to join other British forces heading south to establish blocking positions on the Meuse. In the event, with an improvement in the weather, the Americans contained the enemy. Now under Major General Lewis Bols, the veteran British paratroopers, had arrived in Ostende on Christmas Eve and were concentrated and ready to help in the counter-offensive that was already gaining momentum. Attacking the very tip of the German Bulge, the paratroopers drove the enemy back across the snow covered country during the following weeks. Winter clothing and equipment helped but the Division, as its Allied counterparts, had to learn the skills of winter warfare on the job.

By the middle of January, the Germans were back behind their start lines, with their reserves of men and material further depleted by their offensive. 6th Airborne had been withdrawn to a sector of the line on the River Mass, as they were still needed to hold the front. Their strength, however, was being preserved for the coming Rhine operations. They were the only viable British airborne formation, as 1st Airborne Division was a far from combat effective. Corporal Cooper of 195th Air Landing Field Ambulance recalled the deployment to Holland:

By early February, the danger was over and we were pulled back to a village not far from Antwerp where we spent approximately a week billeted in a private house with a family consisting of a father, mother and two daughters, with whom we had pleasant evenings sitting around the stove. Following this pleasant interlude, we moved into Holland to take over the defence of a line on the River Mass, previously held by the 15th Scottish Division, who we relieved in order for them to take part in exercises for the main amphibious crossing of the Rhine.

In general, the locals were not too friendly, but with the Germans having only recently been driven back across the river and now entrenched on the far bank, they were probably concerned that they might return and take vengeance on those who had been friendly to us.

We had trouble travelling around as many of the roads collapsed, following a thaw and for days at a time nothing heaver than a jeep was allowed to go out. Unfortunately, we didn't know from day to day which roads were closed.

In due course, we in turn were relieved, and returned to our camp in Bulford, where we were granted ten days leave prior to our anticipated participation in the Rhine crossing, which, although no formal announcement had been made, we knew was imminent. Whilst on leave we heard that the Americans had captured intact a railway bridge over the Rhine and we hoped that this might obviate the need for an airborne landing.

With the 6th Airborne Division returned to its camps in February and with preparations underway for the Rhine crossing, there was, however, the Rhineland to clear and parts of the West Wall to overcome before PLUNDER and VARSITY could be launched.

The Winter War

Eisenhower, now fully aware of the German capacity for resistance, prepared operations, delayed by the Battle of the Bulge, to clear the Rhineland as far as the River Rhine. SHAFE planners planned

The damaged bridge at Remagen.

operations that were designed to destroy the main German field forces in the west, before their remnants could withdraw across the great river.

The fighting in early 1945 to reach the Rhine on a front from the Swiss border all the way north to Nijmegen is a subject in itself. In the north, Montgomery's 21st Army Group was to fight a massive and carefully planned battle; using General Crerar's First Canadian Army (Operations VERITIBLE) and General Simpson's Ninth US Army (Operation GRENADE). These operations were designed to reach the Rhine north of the Ruhr, while further south, First US Army's delayed operations to capture the seven Roer dams. With the dams captured, First US Army's operations focused on crossing the River Ruhr and then reaching Rhine around Cologne. Yet further south, Patton's Third US Army was to clear the difficult terrain east of the Ardennes, cross the River Moselle, fight through the Eiffel and reach the central sector of the Rhine between Coblenz and Mannheim.

21st Army Group's shoulder flash.

While General Crerar's First Canadian Army was fighting the main body of the Germans in the west in the Battle of the Rhineland, the US army groups further to the south were approaching the Rhine across greater distances and some equally difficult terrain. First US Army reached the Rhine near Cologne and on 7 March, after several attempts to take a Rhine bridge by *coup de main*, the spearhead of 9th US Armoured Division approached Remargen on the Rhine and found the railway bridge was still standing. With the demolition guard lacking orders to blow the bridge and inadequate explosives, First US Army gained the honour of establishing the first Allied bridgehead across the Rhine. However, the country beyond the Remagen Bridgehead was so unsuitable for offensive operations and without strategically important objectives within striking distance; this was, in reality, a cul-de-sac of little strategic importance. However, it can be argued that the main effect of the Bridge's capture was to draw precious German divisions away from Eisenhower's main effort in the north.

Sergeant Alex Drabik – first man across the Rhine.

The next crossing was further south and was of greater importance. General Omar Bradley, commander 12th US Army Group, received a telephone call on the morning of 23 March at his HQ in Namur from General Patton's Third US Army HQ. His account illustrates the competition and vanity (both British and American) that now bedevilled Eisenhower's command.

General Patton, 'I sneaked a division over last night'.

> *'Brad, don't tell anyone but I'm across.' I replied 'Well I'll be damned – you mean the Rhine?' 'Sure am,' he* [Patton] *replied, I sneaked a division over last night. But there are so few Krauts around they don't know it yet. So don't make any announcement – we'll keep it a secret until we see how it goes.'*

Patton's formal situation report about his crossing at Nierstein pointedly included the statement that this had been achieved '...... without the benefit of aerial bombing, ground smoke, artillery preparation, and airborne assistance, the Third Army at 2200 hours, Thursday evening March 22, crossed the River Rhine.' However, as Bradley recalled. 'That evening Patton telephoned again'.

> *'Brad,' he shouted and his treble voiced trembled, 'for God's sake tell the world we are across. We knocked down thirty-three Krauts* [aircraft] *today when they came after our pontoon bridges. I want the world to know Third Army made it before Monty starts across.'*

General Omar Bradley.

Rhineland Operations of 21st Army Group

Meanwhile, with the limited British involvement on the northern flank of the Battle of the Bulge over, Montgomery turned his attention to Operations VERITABLE and GRENADE. He described the aims of the fighting west of the Rhine to close up to the great waterway between Xanten and Nijmegen.

> *The object of the battle of the Rhineland was to destroy all enemy forces between the Rhine and the Meuse from the Nijmegen bridgehead as far south as the general line Julich-Düsseldorf, and*

subsequently to line up along the west bank of the Rhine with the Ninth US Army from Düüsseldorf to Moers, Second [British] Army from Moers to Rees and [First] Canadian Army from exclusive Rees to Nijmegen.

This was to be achieved by First Canadian Army, with British formations under command, in Operation VERITABLE; an attack south-east from the Groesbeek

Field marshall Montgomery

Heights near Nijmegen, which had been seized during MARKET GARDEN in September 1944. The Canadian's immediate objectives were the breaching of the West Wall's defences and clearance of the Reichswald. Subsequently, they were to take the defended towns of Udem and Goch before heading south-east to Geldern and Xanten where they would link up with Ninth US Army, who, in Operation GRENADE, would be advancing in a north-easterly direction.

Facing 21st Army Group was *General* Schlemm, commander of the First *Fallschirmjäger* Army. He was experienced in holding operations, having been schooled in the art, in the resource starved Italian theatre. Here he learnt to utilise terrain to maximise his defensive effect. However, on the Rhine, Schlemm recounted that his orders were to hold the ground come what may:

General **Schlemm.**

Once the battle was joined, it was obvious that I no longer had a free hand in the conduct of the defence. My orders were that under no circumstances was any land between the Maas and the Rhine to be given up without permission of the Commander in Chief West, von Rundstedt, who in turn had to ask Hitler. For every withdrawal that I was forced to make due to an Allied attack, I had to send back a detailed explanation.

Even so, Schlemm and other German commanders repeatedly requested that they be allowed to fall back to the Rhine where they could adopt strongly held positions. Instead Hitler kept eighty-five divisions fighting west of the Rhine, forbidding any withdrawal and threatening to execute commanders who lost a bridge intact.

Starting on 8th February 1945, VERITABLE and its continuation BLOCKBUSTER is characterised by Brigadier Essame of 43rd Wessex Division as:

16

...... lasting for twenty eight days and nights in almost unspeakable conditions of flood, mud and misery. The troops were soaked with almost incessant rain; there was no escaping it and no shelter. We met the First Parachute Army, the last remaining German indoctrinated youth, fighting with undiminished courage on German soil supported by 700 mortars and almost a thousand guns, on virtually equal terms.

Fighting through the northern extensions of the Siegfried Line, which the Germans had five months to work on since the failure of MARKET GARDEN, was a costly business. The densely wooded and heavily fortified Reichswald, the defended towns, such as Udem and Goch, and the positions in depth (the Hochwald Layback) took a month to fight through. The level of destruction of the German homeland, as he entered the ruins of Cleve, was recorded by a veteran member of 4th Wiltshires:

There were craters and fallen trees everywhere, bomb craters packed so tight that the debris from one was piled against the rim of the next in a pathetic heap of rubble, roofs and radiators. There was not an undamaged house anywhere, piles of smashed furniture, clothing, children's' books and toys, everything, was spilled in hopeless confusion amidst the bombed skeletons of the town.

Infantry from Canada, the West Country, Wales and Scotland bore the brunt of the costly fighting through the ruined towns and the sodden German countryside.

General Simpson's Ninth US Army was formally under

operational command of 21st Army Group for the clearance of the Rhineland in operation GRENADE, but the degree of influence Montgomery was able to exert by this stage over US forces under his command was strictly limited. Simpson's objective was the seizure of the Rhine's western bank, from where his army would, in subsequent operations, strike at the northern edge of the Ruhr. However, delays in starting his attack resulted from floodwaters in the river valley and First US Army's failure to capture the Roer Dams in some very difficult mountainous terrain. Without the dams being secured, there was a very real threat that the Germans could

General Simpson, Commander Ninth US Army.

release millions of gallons of water, and isolate a Ninth US Army bridgehead, which would, consequently, be vulnerable to destruction. In the event, to prevent an attack across the Roer, the Germans, however, released the water from the Schwammenauel Dam which flooded the river valley and formed an obstacle that prevented the Ninth Army advance. Eventually, after a two week delay, with the worst of the flood waters receding, six US divisions launched a surprise assault crossing over the still violent river on 24 February 1945, preceded by a massive forty-five minute bombardment by over 1,500 guns. During the delay caused by the flooding, nine German divisions had been sucked away from the US front, north to the bitter VERITABLE battle being fought by General Crerar's troops. This contributed to the US assault divisions losing fewer than a hundred men killed in action on the first day of the assault.

Ninth Army's badge.

With VERITABLE, GRENADE and the advance of the First US Army underway, a programme of air operations on a large scale was conducted by the Allied tactical and bomber commands. 'This was designed to weaken the German defence as a whole, and to assist 21st Army Group and 12th Army Group in particular, by the isolation and reduction of the Ruhr's war-making capacity.' According to the British Official History, the principal aims were, firstly:

> ... to isolate the Ruhr from central and southern Germany by cutting the main railways..., secondly, to attack continuously west of that line the enemy's communications and transport system; and, thirdly, to prepare the battle area for the impending Rhine crossing by 21st Army Group.

The official historian concluded that: 'In the next few weeks much of the industrial power of the Ruhr was dissipated in the dust of explosions from a rain of bombs which fell almost daily from the air'.

Meanwhile, Simpson drove his men on to the Rhine and with massive US material strength, his divisions poured over the Roer by nineteen pontoon bridges and:

> The enemy's resistance was soon characteristic of a general retreat in which only an attempt could be made to delay the Allied advance by holding road junctions and communications centres in key towns or villages, using in each case a number of assault and

anti-aircraft guns and mortars and groups of supporting infantry.

As planned, the 35th US Division met up with Montgomery's 53rd Welsh Division at Geldern at mid-afternoon on 3 March and together the armies advanced east, squeezing the remains of fifteen German divisions belonging to First *Fallschrimjager* Army, into a rapidly reducing bridgehead. Hitler would still not sanction their withdrawal despite General Schlemm's protestations. In his post war interrogation, he commented that once he was hemmed in to a shrinking bridgehead whose perimeter ran from Xanten, the Bonninghardtwald and down to the Rhine at Moers: 'I could see my hopes for a long life rapidly dwindling, since I had nine bridges in my sector!' A verbatim note in the Führer Conference records, gives Hitler's reasoning in response to a suggestion that they redeploy east of the Rhine. 'I want him to hang on to the West Wall as long as is humanly possible, since withdrawal would merely mean moving the catastrophe from one place to another.'

Eventually, with Hitler's threat of execution hanging over him, Schlemm authorised, on his own initiative, the withdrawal of what manpower he could save before blowing the Wesel bridges. On 5 March 1945, Montgomery's armies reached the Rhine in the area chosen for the crossing of the great River, having suffered a total of 23,000 casualties in First Canadian and Ninth US Armies.

The Battle of the Rhineland had cost General Schlemm's First *Fallschirmjäger* Army between 90,000 and 100,000 men, with casualties being largely concentrated amongst nineteen infantry divisions, which, in many cases, were now reduced little more than cadres. Altogether fighting west of the Rhine cost von Rundstedt, C-in-C West, half a

Hitler used the threat of execution to bolster his commanders' determination to hold ground west of the Rhine.

million men and, for the third time, his job. At the age of seventy, however, he could finally retire knowing that he had delayed the enemy more successfully than any other commander and that the end would be not long in coming.

The Strategic Situation

It is widely accepted that Hitler's decision to remain fighting west of the Rhine, was a major mistake that probably shortened the war by a few weeks, compounding earlier errors. By gathering the majority of his best troops for the Ardennes offensive, Hitler had also left Germany open to the Soviet Winter offensive launched by Zhukov and Koniev. In the east, facing a five to one superiority in men and materiel, the German armies collapsed and the Red Army, driven on by Stalin's threats, advanced some 250 miles to within forty miles of Berlin, where running out of steam they were eventually halted by last ditch German resistance. Meanwhile, at the Yalta Conference, the Allies were only able to report to Stalin that they had restored their lines of the previous November.

The Ardennes offensive had cost Hitler his last strategic and operational reserves. With, in addition, the losses suffered during the Rhineland Battles, the *Wehrmacht* was in March 1945 only

A pair of 6th Airborne Division's signallers in Holland in early 1945.

Montgomery and Senior Allied Commanders show Prime Minister Churchill around a captured section of Hitler's West Wall.

capable of standing on the defensive. As Eisenhower wrote, with the benefit of hindsight'... the enemy was now in no condition to hold fast in the defended line to which he had been compelled to retreat'. The end indeed would not be long in coming but the Rhine and the heavily defended Ruhr would first have to be overcome to defeat Germany.

Second British Army

At the end of Operation VERITABLE, after nine months of active campaigning, the British Army that had crossed the German frontline and was about to take part in the last major Allied offensive of the war, was very different from the army that had landed in Normandy. Brigadier Essame of 43rd Wessex Division wrote of the state of the British Second Army at the end of March 1945:

> *Despite exposure twenty-four hours a day for over a month, to the almost incessant rain and sleet and intense and sustained enemy fire, the morale of the British troops as the battle progressed rose, rather than declined, to a higher level than at any stage during the campaign.*

This seemingly counter intuitive statement is supported by the fact that the number of Second Army soldiers reporting sick was at an

all time low in February and March 1944 and the incidence of psychiatric casualties had declined markedly. Essame accounts for this phenomenon as '... men, the majority of whom had been new to the horrors of the battlefield in Normandy, had now got into their stride and had become inured to the sights and smells of battle.'

Men of 6th Airbourne Division Headquarters.

Not only were Montgomery's troops in a better mental and physical shape but they had become experienced campaigners. 6th Airborne Division, though having suffered heavy casualties in Normandy, was skilled in the art of war and its officers knew their business. During the autumn training exercises in the UK, commanders who had proved themselves in battle were promoted and cut their teeth in their new roles in the Ardennes.

Ordinary infantry soldiers who joined 6th Airborne as casualty replacements, and had impressed in battle, wanted to stay with the Division (having survived long enough to bond with their comrades, most wanted to stay) and were sent on parachute training, where they were joined by individual soldiers from the Airlanding Brigade, who had volunteered to undergo parachute training. Officers and men returning to duty having recovered from wounds also stiffened the Division. 6th Airborne Division was at its zenith in terms of experience and military efficiency.

Costly though the Rhineland battles had been, the British, American and Canadian armies were well led and their soldiers had endured the worst of the winter. With replacements swelling their ranks, they knew that victory was inevitable, despite the motivational cautioning of their officers about the battles to come. With logistic superiority and air supremacy to support them, the only real question was when it all would end. Conversely, the Germans after, the Battle of the Bulge and the losses suffered facing VERITABLE and GRENADE, were in a parlous state.

CHAPTER TWO

The German Defenders

Defeated in Normandy, the Germans belatedly took measures to put their economy and nation onto a total war footing. Places of entertainment were closed, non-essential activities curtailed and men and women were directed into key industries and into the *Wehrmacht*. Within the forces, as already mentioned, men were taken from the now largely redundant *Kriegsmarine* and from the bloated ranks of the Goering's *Luftwaffe*. The only units spared were the manpower intensive anti-aircraft commands. Never the less, the resulting regeneration of units was spectacular. Divisions such as the 84th Infantry, who Second Army was to face on the banks of the Rhine, had been reconstituted as a *volksgrenadier* division, following its virtual destruction at Falaise. Germany's armoured vehicle production had also reached a peak, despite the best efforts of the Allied bomber offensive. Reconstituted, the best of the formations were sent to the West Wall along with two thirds of the armoured rolling off production lines.

Despite rebuilding the *Wehrmacht* in a matter of months, this was not the same quality of Army as before, being made up of a high proportion of men who would previously have been regarded as too old, too young or had a physical infirmity that would have excluded them from service. The better 'divisions', in many cases, consisted of two regiments (equivalent to a British brigade) each of two infantry battalions with little transport. Artillery was short but this deficiency was made up by significant numbers of mortars and multi-barrel rocket launchers; the *nebelwerfer*, which was the major cause of allied casualties. German small arms firepower, was however, largely undiminished with a generous allocation of MG 34 and MG 42 *Spandaus* in infantry units.

Volkssturm

The poorer quality formations were based on the *volkssturm*; the old and sick men of the German Home Guard, with in some cases their only uniform being an arm band. The commanding officer of 41st *Volkssturm* Battalion described an event when his unit was sent into battle early in March. Although an extreme case, his story is generally representative of what happened to many battalions such as his.

I had 400 men in my battalion and we were ordered to go into the line in our civilian clothes. I told the local Party Leader that I could not accept the responsibility of leading men into battle without uniforms or training. Just before commitment the unit was given 180 Danish rifles, but there was no ammunition. We also had four machine guns and 100 Panzerfausts. None of the men had received any training in firing a machine gun, and they were all afraid of handling the anti-tank weapon. Although my men were quite ready to help their country, they refused to go into battle without uniforms and without training.

A member of the *Hitlerjugend* ready with his panzerschrek; a copy of the US Bazooka.

What can a volkssturm *man do with a rifle without ammunition! The men went home. That was the only thing they could do.*

The smaller one shot disposable *Panzerfaust* easily used by any soldier with a bit of nerve.

The Hitler Youth

The younger soldiers recruited from the *Hitlerjugend* (HJ) movement, despite their lack of age, were often good and dedicated material. However, in the Ardennes the *Volksgrenadier* divisions' HJ recruits had not performed to their potential, as the Normandy veterans and older *Volkssturm* knew it was 'all up for Germany' and encouraged the boys – for that is what they were

24

– to surrender. Consequently, it was decided to keep HJ conscripts, some of whom were boys as young as twelve years of age, in separate units, rarely more than a hundred strong.

By keeping the boys in their own HJ units, with fanatical Nazi leadership, the Nazis were able to exploit the years of indoctrination, along with the innate bravery of youth that makes warfare a young man's game. Many went willingly, with patriotism and the gullibility of youth; believing Göbels's propaganda that Hitler's 'victory weapons' and one last push would turn the tide and ultimately deliver victory to the Fatherland. Of all the deceptions perpetrated by the Nazis on the German people, this was possibly the most cynical and evil exploitation of them all.

Even though they had little formal recruit training, during compulsory HJ service they had received, along with Nazi indoctrination, years of military training during routine HJ meetings and camps. This 'training', with weapons and ammunition, often re-enacting German victories earlier in the war, laid a solid military foundation. In reality, however, as with the *Volksturm*, they lacked weapons and equipment but the spirit was willing and HJ units from the Rhineland, were prepared to defend their home towns with whatever they had. *Panzerfausts*, in particular, proved to be an effective weapon even in the hands of novices, who were often referred to, by the Allies as 'bazooka boys'.

Fallschirmjäger

With the SS panzer divisions, now deployed to the east to stem the Russian offensive, the *Fallschirmjäger* alone in the west,

Youngsters were fooled into believing that their *Führer* could still win the war for Germany through the employment of new wonder weapons. Thus encouraged they fought on like men. This very young NCO has the Iron Cross.

A much decorated _Fallschirmjäger_ NCO and men pose behind a tripod mounted MG42.

retained much of their former quality. The latter provided the backbone of the German defences in the Rhineland and were the major opponents of the British and Canadian forces during VERITABLE and BLOCKBUSTER. Mostly aged under twenty-five, these troops were parachutists in name only, few having been trained to jump but nurtured on the deeds of their forebears at Crete, Cassino, etc. they had an _esprit de corps_ that most of the _Wehrmacht_ had long since lost. Also, with many of their recruits coming from _Luftwaffe_ stations, they had not tasted the bitter pill of defeat and their tenacity in the fighting in early 1945 may have had a lot to do with the fact that only unconditional German surrender was on the table and they had little choice but to continue resisting.

Veteran _Fallschirmjäger,_ and persistent thorn in the Allied side, _Oberstleutnant_ von der Hydte left the text of his early 1945 speech to new recruits joining his regiment:

> _I demand of every soldier the renunciation of all personal wishes. Whoever swears on the Prussian flag has no right to personal possessions! From the moment he enlists in the_ Fallschirmjäger _and comes to my regiment, every soldier enters the new order of humanity and gives up everything he possessed before and which is outside the new order. There is only one law henceforth for him – the law of our unit. He must abjure every weaker facet of his own character, all personal ambition, and every personal desire. From the renunciation of the individual, the true personality of the soldier arises. Every member of the regiment must know what he is fighting for._
>
> _He must be quite convinced that this struggle is a struggle for the existence of the whole German nation and that no other ending of this battle is possible than that of the victory of German arms. ... He must_

26

learn to believe in victory even when at certain moments logical thinking scarcely makes a German victory seem possible. ...Only the soldier who is schooled in philosophy and believes in his political faith implicitly can fight as this war demands that he shall fight. ...lack of this faith is the reason why so many German infantry divisions have been destroyed.

In summary, despite the presence of the committed *Fallschirmjäger*, overall the *Wehrmacht*, as demonstrated by the Ardennes offensive, was no longer capable of successfully mounting major offensive operations. There were too few first class formations, panzer divisions were largely 'armoured' in name only and, of course, the Allies were no longer the bemused armies of 1940 that were so easily overwhelmed by Hitler's *blitzkrieg*.

XLVII Panzerkorps

XLVII *Panzerkorps* was deployed in reserve, well to the east of the German defensive positions on the Rhine, with 15th Panzer Grenadiers in the north and 116th Panzer in the south opposite what was to be the American sector. 116th *Windhund* Panzer Division was assessed by allied intelligence on 22 March, as having up to seventy tanks, while 15th Panzer Grenadier Division was believed to hold fifteen panzers and twenty to thirty assault guns.

Both formations were veteran, still commanded by professional officers and had as much equipment as any German armoured formation that was still fighting. They had prepared sundry counter-attack plans and had thoroughly rehearsed all of the deployment options.

An SD KFZ 251 armoured half-track bearing the 'Greyhound' badge of 116th Panzer Division

Defence on the Rhine

Charged with holding the Rhine, as Hitler's new C-in-C West, was the stocky, blunt jawed and resolute *Feldmarschall* Albert Kesselring. He had gained a reputation as a defensive genius

fighting delaying actions in Italy on the Gustav and Gothic Lines. Arriving at his new headquarters he reputedly announced to his staff 'Well gentlemen, I am the new V3'. On the Rhine, the policy 'Laughing Albert' had to implement, remained focussed on the defence of the Ruhr, which with the loss of Upper Silesia to the Russians, was the last industrial area, vital to sustain German forces in action. To achieve this, Kesselring had nominally sixty-five divisions but in reality they totalled less than half this number.

Feldmarschall Albert Kesselring.

Despite an acute weapons shortage and the seemingly crippling blows that German industry and communications were receiving from the Allied air forces, Kesselring managed to put together a creditable defence to oppose the expected assault crossing of the Rhine. However, this defence was less strong than Montgomery believed he would encounter; a Leliet which was based on his experience of the bitter fighting west of the Rhine.

General Schlemm's First *Fallschirmjäger Armie* remained responsible for the sector opposite 21st Army Group, including the Xanten – Wesel sector. During his post war interrogation Schlemm explained that:

> … *A parachute drop over the Rhine was considered inevitable, and efforts were made to determine the most probable spot.*

Schlemm had a captured Allied report analyzing the parachute drop at Arnhem in September 1944, and from this document, he learnt that Allied views were now against a paratroop landing too far away from the ground troops destined to contact it. By plotting the areas that were topographically suitable for a parachute drop and near the Rhine, Schlemm claims the most likely area seemed to be just east of Wesel. It was in this neighbourhood that he therefore expected the crossing attempt would be made.

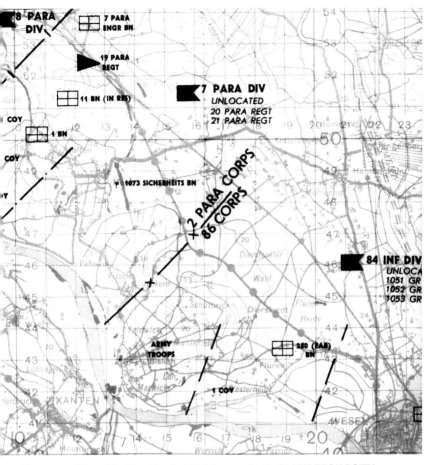

Enemy positions identified by Second Army prior to PLUNDER/VARSITY.

Schlemm's views, however, were not considered sound by his superiors at Army Group H, by *Feldmarschall* Von Rundstedt or his successor:

> ...*The expected northern crossing was to take place, according to these latter opinions, in the neighbourhood of Emmerich. The assault would be directed north-east and designed to take the Ijssel line in the rear. Since this was to be the big attack, Schlemm was ordered to send a large part of his artillery to the Twenty-Fifth Army who would be faced with this new offensive...*

As subsequent events will prove, this was a miscalculation of some significance and Schlemm's deployment on the Rhine with two

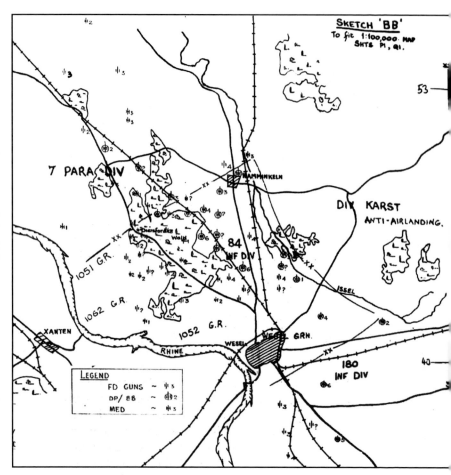

A diagram from the post operational report showing the German artillery batteries in the VARSITY area.

corps and an armoured reserve was, as was the case with the Germans pre-D Day dispositions, a compromise. II *Fallschirmjäger Korps* were deployed in the north, with 6, 7 and 8 *Fallschirmjäger* Divisions astride the town of Rees. In what was to become the left assault sector of Second British Army, Schlemm had deployed General Straube's LXXXVI *Korps* centred on Wesel, with 84th and 180th Divisions under command. While Schlemm's armoured counter-attack reserve, XLVII *Panzerkorps*, was located fifteen miles to the north-east of Emmerich.

The divisions directly facing the British assault were 8th *Fallschirmjäger* and 84th Infantry Division. 7th *Fallschirmjäger* Division had not been properly located but some of its units were known to be well forward. The former was on the left of II *Fallschirmjäger Korps* and had lost heavily in the fighting west of the Rhine and when it withdrew across the line in early March, it had an infantry strength of just 900 men. 84th Division, a luckless formation under the command of *Generalmajor* Fiebig, had been virtually destroyed, for the second time, at the beginning of VERITABLE, and was assessed on 12 March, as having a strength of just 500 infantrymen. However, it was in the process of being reconstituted a when PLUNDER started on the night of 23/24 March. Amongst those who had already arrived to join the beleaguered division were some *Volkstrum* (German Home Guard), some static *Wehrkreis* (German military district) troops, including 317 *Ersatz* Battalion in Wesel and those troops encountered around Bislich and, amongst others, 286th Ear Battalion, made up of soldiers who were deaf or hard of hearing.

One formation that the Allies had little information on was *Kampfgruppe Karst* . It is not clear whether or not the half-tracks, armoured cars and light armour had been identified before the operation and included in the armoured totals listed in Second Army's intelligence summaries but what had been missed was that its specific role was anti-airlanding. This was crucial for the two allied airborne divisions of XVIII US Airborne Corps, as it was German tactical doctrine to drive into the heart of an airborne drop, seeking to disrupt the enemy while he was at his most vulnerable, i.e. before he could assemble and receive all of his heavier weapons. *Kampfgruppe Karst* was located to the east of the River Issel; exactly where Schlem had assessed the Allies would

Luftwaffe field troops dug-in to protect 88mm gun deployed in the anti-tank role.

deploy their airborne forces. Even though they were, in the event, just the wrong side of the Issel they were well placed to be in operation against the Allies.

Look at it properly!

That is the latest German amphibian tank having still stronger armour plates than the well-known „Royal Tiger". Its firing capacity surpasses everything known so far. It simply vomits fire.
The funny part about it is that it can swim. It does not bother about the inundations caused by us.

At any moment it may emerge in front of your positions, but you have to hold out.

Don't think the German offensive was launched in those few places only. That was only the beginning.
We have already advanced a nice bit in Belgium and it has proved an irresistible advance. The fog which undoubtedly favoured us at the outset but rendered operations more difficult later on has disappeared. Ever since we have been making headway.
On the other hand your airmen are again in a position to drop their Teddar carpets in order to plaster our tank spearheads. They are indefatigable in their endeavours for everything depends upon their efforts. But their losses are tremendous. It goes without saying that many of our own tanks have been put out of action by allied bombers crashing in great numbers with their bomb loads. One notices at once the reappearance of the Luftwaffe which is of vital importance to our spearheads. You have certainly observed the withdrawal of certain units from comparatively quiet sectors of the front in order to strengthen the fighting forces in the new battle area.
As a result your own positions will be weakened. But you must be prepared to face our attack all the same. Unfortunately you have little or nothing to oppose our assault.
And all this because those bragging American fellows meant to march to Berlin on their own. Now where they are getting a proper hiding you have to pay for it and have to come to their aid. Perhaps you will already move to-morrow? You never know in advance!
It would be better for you to remain where you are now considering that you have established yourself fairly well. And you won't miss anything by remaining where you are because sooner or later you'll be able to see the latest German amphibian tank when it emerges in front of your position.
That will be a nice surprise for you!

Look at it properly !
...... if not to-day, to-morrow.

A German propoganda leaflet designed to undermine Allied morale.

When studying the operation in January 1945, Second British Army Commanders stated that they expected to face up to 58,000 German troops, with 16,000 infantry occupying defensive positions on the river line, within the assault area. It was assumed that while the Germans stood and fought west of the Rhine, they would be bound to be preparing defences to protect the northern flank of the vital Ruhr, which Allied intelligence believed would in due course be occupied by enemy forces withdrawing east of the river. There are no firm numbers but following the German losses during VERITABLE, there can have been fewer than 7,000 infantry of a lower quality than expected dug in on the banks of the Rhine in the crossing area.

Flak was the one weapon system that the Germans had positioned along the Rhine in relative abundance, as they were expecting an airborne operation in support of an assault crossing. Deployed in and around what were to become the VARSITY drop zones, were 114 heavy and 712 light anti-aircraft guns. As we will see, the abundance of flak and its effect on the airborne assault, is an indication of what could have happened on a much larger scale if Hitler had decided against fighting west of the Rhine.

Few elements of the ground defence had been accurately located prior to the assault of 23/24 March. This was because intelligence was limited to air photography, electronic intelligence and artillery sound ranging and without an active SOE network or a resistance organization to pass on ground information, units in buildings and woods were difficult to identify. In addition, the *ad hoc* nature of the German defence made it difficult for intelligence officers to construct a meaningful picture of the German Order of Battle.

A Royal Engineer post action report on the tactical deployment of the enemy encountered on the Rhine reads:

> *Enemy ground defences in the area of the proposed crossing were not highly developed. In the main they were directed towards the protection of likely crossing points, larger villages and towns, and there was no continuous defensive line along the river. Defences mainly consisted of field positions defended buildings, all with little wire and few mines. However, where possible the Germans had flooded areas sufficiently well to make them obstacles to armour or at least very difficult going. There was little depth in the German defences.*

General Walter Blumentritt.

However, fearing the worst, the Allies were forced to prepare plans for a deliberate assault crossing of the Rhine, based on the fact that troops during an amphibious operation would be extremely vulnerable and that the balance would favour the German defenders. During planning an airborne drop (Operation VARSITY) was considered essential to unhinge German resistance on the Rhine. In addition, they fully appreciated the German ability to mount effective counter-attacks with *ad hoc* forces and understood that it was a dangerous part of the German operational art. As with the Normandy D Day, the Allies would need to apply superior numbers and an integrated fire plan from ground and from the air. Special equipment and well-prepared troops were needed to ensure that the enemy were overcome. This would provide a springboard for 21st Army Group's drive into the heart of Germany.

On 21 March, the Germans suffered another blow, when the redoubtable General Schlemm's headquarters of First *Fallschirmjäger* Army was located by Allied intelligence and in the resulting air strike, Schlemm was badly wounded. The general called forward to take his place was General Walter Blumentritt who had been von Rundstedt's chief of staff and following his erstwhile commanders final dismissal, was now available for re-employment.

CHAPTER THREE

Planning and Preparation

With the Allies having closed up to the Rhine in March 1945, there was to be no single thrust across the great river but a series of attempts to cross, on a broad front, before launching the final offensive from the resulting bridgeheads into the heart of Germany.

Though often dismissed by the likes of Patton, as '… more of a politician than a general', Eisenhower maintained a focus on his immediate aim; the elimination of the Ruhr as the heart of Germany's war fighting capability. He placed the Anglo American main-effort in the north, under the command of the master of the deliberate attack; Montgomery. The commitment of an airborne corps to Montgomery is confirmation that this was to be the main effort.

With what he was confident would be an assured crossing north of the Ruhr, Eisenhower justifiably believed that further south, the other US Armies would be able to 'bounce the Rhine' where it was narrower and less well defended. The Supreme Commander was in effect playing to the strengths and qualities of his army commanders and the nature of the soldiers under their command.

Planning for the Rhine crossing and final campaign began well before the New Year, with the issue of directives. With the Ninth US Army and XVIII US Airborne Corps under command of Montgomery's 21st Army Group, a force of British, American and Canadians would carry out a deliberate assault crossing of the Rhine, north of the Ruhr aimed at isolating and taking the vital industrial area. To complete the envelopment of the Ruhr from the south, First US Army, who had already captured the bridge at Remargen would advance in a north-easterly direction.

While General Crerar's First Canadian Army was fighting the Battle of the Rhineland, General Dempsey's uncommitted Second Army HQ prepared the deliberate crossing of the river with both

General Dempsey.

overwhelming numbers and overwhelming resources. By early February they had produced a study of the tasks involved in an assault crossing of the Rhine and airborne drop. This study was sub-divided into the four major parts: 'The assumptions on which the subsequent corps study was to be based on, intelligence, problems relating to the crossing, engineer tasks and maintenance (logistic) problems'. With this ground work established, the task of conducting a corps study and developing the assault method was allocated to XII Corps who had been relieved of operational tasks and moved to an approximately similar piece of terrain on the River Maas south of Maastricht.

XVIII US Airborne Corps, who had yet to conduct an operation for the Allied Airborne Army, consisting of 6th British and 17th US Airborne Divisions, was nominated to plan airborne aspects of PLUNDER in their own sub-operation, code named VARSITY. This account concentrates on the operations of 6th Airborne Division. Great care was taken to integrate the airborne plan into the assault river crossing operations, thus addressing another of the MARKET GARDEN failings.

Ground

For the planning of PLUNDER and VARSITY, considerable data was made available from a wide variety of sources, regarding the river's flood plain, the flood dykes, the approaches to the river banks, the average water level and sundry other detail necessary to prepare an amphibious plan.

The river in this sector was on average 300 yards wide, with certain sectors being up to 500 yards. The current flowed at an average speed of 3 knots opposite Wesel. At its narrowest point this stretch of the Rhine was twice the width of the location where Patton had successfully sneaked across on the night of 22/23 March 1945 and an altogether more challenging obstacle. While British and American engineers were able to examine the home bank and select entry points into the river, there was a degree of uncertainty about the state of the bank on the far side and its suitability for amphibious armour.

The area north of the Dieserfordterwald, including the bridges across the River Issel, where the two divisions of XVIII US Airborne Corps were to drop, was more easily analysed by conventional air photography and maps. Up to seven miles from the Rhine, it was a relatively open area but dominated on its fringes by large wooded

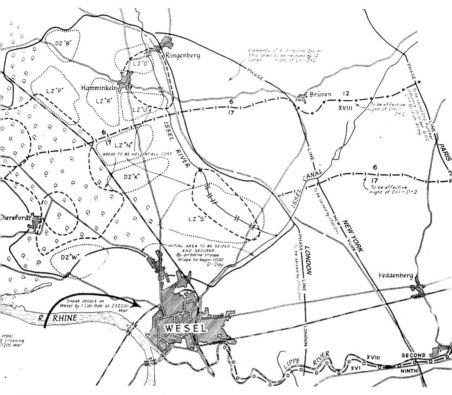

XVIII US Airborne Corp's Varsity area and plan.

areas and the significant village Hamminkeln, in the British area. Sources information regarding the bridges across the Issel were the subject of much analysis to produce briefing material for Airlanding battalions of 6th Airborne Division.

Resources

As 21st Army Group was Eisenhower's main effort, allocation of manpower and logistic resources, in contrast to the MARKET GARDEN campaign, were generous enough not only to be able to get across a heavily defended strategic barrier of the Rhine but to take the battle into the heart of Germany. Eisenhower, during the planning phase, envisaged that 21st Army Group would strike east 'from the Lower Rhine north of the Ruhr and into the North German Plain' because this route offered the most suitable terrain for mobile operations … [and] … the quickest means of denying the Germans the vital Ruhr industries'.

Material and stores of all natures flowed into the newly opened

Army Road Head, which was sited in the wrecked country of the former Operation VERITABLE battle area. Into this area troops poured, not only to establish the logistic infrastructure but for training. Massive traffic circuits and dumps were laid out. The scale of the preparations was massive; 30,000 tons of engineer materiel was piled for miles along the road north from Goch, with an additional tonnage pre-loaded on 940 vehicles. 60,000 tons ammunition was stacked along ten miles of the north-south road just east of the Maas and 28,000 tons of combat supplies were dumped around the ruined town of Kevlaer, its rubble being used to create areas of hard standing.

All this activity presented problems of concealment that were considered by HQ Second Army to be 'somewhat similar to those met in the UK before Operation Neptune', except that German patrols could cross the river to look for evidence of dumping of bridging stores and other preparations of the home bank. Second Army reported that 'The planners accepted that it was impossible to conceal from the enemy the fact that 21st Army Group intended to assault the Rhine north of the Ruhr, but great care was taken to ensure that the date and place of assault were not prejudiced'. RE Camouflage companies laboured to conceal the preparations and their effectiveness was confirmed by an RAF recce sortie launched on D-1, which could find no evidence that would lead German aircraft and photo interpreters to identify the location of the coming assault.

21st Army Group Plan

For Operation PLUNDER, 21st Army Group comprised three armies; Ninth US Army, Second British Army and First Canadian Army. The assaults by Second and Ninth Armies would be launched simultaneously.

The task of Ninth US Army was, to mount an assault crossing of the Rhine in the area of Rheinberg and to secure a bridgehead from the junction of the Ruhr and Rhine rivers to Bottrop and Dorsten. Thereafter, General Simpson was to be prepared to advance to a line inclusive of Hamm and Munster. Their tasks also included the protection of the right flank of Second British Army and the vital bridging sites at Wesel.

Second British Army was to assault the Rhine in the area of Xanten and Rees and to establish a bridgehead between Rees and

Wesel and subsequently advance on a three corps front north-east towards the town of Rheine.

Initially the task of First Canadian Army was to assist in broadening the frontage of Second Army's assault by carrying out feint attacks along the Rhine on their left flank, while holding securely the line of the rivers Rhine and Maas from Emmerich westwards to the sea. The Canadians were, however, represented in the assault phase by 9th Canadian Infantry Brigade. Made up of Canadian highland battalions, such as the North Nova Scotia Highlanders, they were attached to 51st Highland Division, as a forth brigade. Later First Canadian Army was to be prepared to advance into eastern Holland and to protect the left flank of Second Army.

Air Operations

With some difficulty, the Allied 'Bomber Barons' were prevailed upon to coordinate their activities with that of the Army. The air forces would have rather continued to concentrate on the 'THUNDERCLAP Plan', which was designed to deliver a sudden and catastrophic blow by bombing Berlin, Dresden, Chemnitz and Leipzig, with a view to bringing about Germany's surrender. The

All three Armies of 21st Army Group were to take part in the Rhine crossing. Montgomery, Eisenhower and Bradley seen here just before it took place.

support needed by the ground forces required the bomber commanders to carry out a comprehensive programme of

interdiction sorties in support of PLUNDER; the 'Ruhr Plan'. Ninth Tactical Air Force was tasked to isolate the area north of the Ruhr and prevent the movement of German reserves to the battlefield. As the three railway lines in the area had already been heavily bombed, it would, therefore, concentrate on the sixteen most significant bridges giving access to the battle area. However, as a part of their attempt to bomb Germany into submission, the air forces tripled the tonnage of bombs requested by the armies, with the result that the final advance across northern Germany was often slowed by the over generous results of earlier bomber sorties.

The blue crusader's cross of Dempsey's Second Army.

Second British Army's Plan

After much study, the plan that was eventually arrived at called for an assault on a frontage of two corps (XII and XXX Corps) with a planned D Day being the night of 23/24 March 1945. In outline, the plan made by General Dempsey, commander Second Army, was to assault with two corps:

RIGHT XII Corps, LEFT XXX Corps, each with one division up. VIII Corps was to hold securely the West bank of the R RHINE during the concentration period until the assault corps were ready to assume control of divisions holding the river line immediately before the assault.

XVIII US Airborne Corps was to be dropped east of the R RHINE after the river assaults had taken place. The principles for its employment were that it should drop within range of artillery sited on the West bank of the R RHINE and that the link up with the ground forces should take place on D Day.

To release Headquarters XVIII US Airborne Corps as soon as possible, Headquarters VIII Corps was to take over from that corps within seven days.

Second Army would then be correctly positioned to continue the advance into the North German plains with VIII Corps RIGHT, XII Corps CENTRE and XXX Corps LEFT.

II Canadian Corps was to be passed through the LEFT of

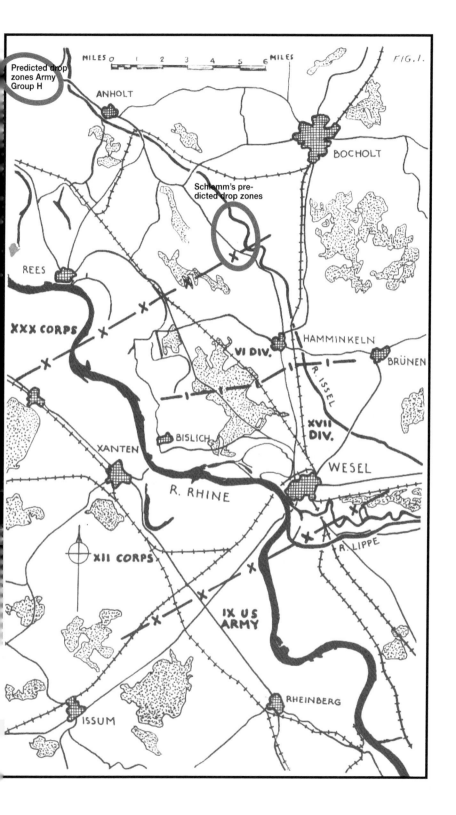

FIG.1.

MILES 0 1 2 3 4 5 6 MILES

Predicted drop zones Army Group H

ANHOLT

BOCHOLT

Schlemm's pre-dicted drop zones

REES

XXX CORPS

HAMMINKELN

VI DIV.

BRÜNEN

R. ISSEL

BISLICH

XVII DIV.

XANTEN

WESEL

R. RHINE

XII CORPS

R. LIPPE

IX US ARMY

ISSUM

RHEINBERG

Second Army bridgehead and handed back to First Canadian Army when it was in a position to exercise command.

In the first phase of Second Army's plan, the two assault divisions were to capture the low-lying ground east of the river up to approximately the line of the Wesel – Emmrich railway. XXX Corps would begin the attack on the left flank, astride Rees, at 2100 hours on 23 March, with 1 Commando Brigade crossing the Rhine to seize Wesel an hour later, while XII Corps would be led by 15th Scottish Division's assault from the area of Xanten at 0200 hours. At the same time, XVI US Corps would launch their amphibious attack south of Wesel. The second phase was to be the capture of the Issel bridges, with or without the assistance of XVIII US Airborne Corps (scheduled for 1000 hours on 24 March), as they could easily be prevented from dropping by poor weather. By the time they launched the assault, Second Army were confident that they could, indeed capture the bridges unaided if necessary, all be it in slower time and with greater casualties. The breakout on to the North German Plain would be Phase Three of the operation.

With the fighting on the west bank of the Rhine having finally ended on 11 March, there was less than two weeks to complete the planning, deployment and implementation of the largest and most complex amphibious and airborne operation since the Normandy landings. This was a tall order but after nine months of campaigning the Allied planning staffs were up to the challenge.

Enemy

The area that 6th Airborne Division was about to drop into, was held by 84th *Volksgrenadier* Division, commanded by *Generalmajor* Fiebig, who was later described by his captors as being 'a charming officer who it would seem to be more at home at a cocktail party than as a divisional commander'. In his post war interrogation, it was clear that *Generalmajor* Fiebig shared some of his commander's views about the likelihood of an airborne landing in his area of responsibility. He:

> ... *claimed that the Germans were not unaware of our preparations for an airborne operation in support of the Rhine crossings and appreciated that no fewer than four allied airborne divisions were available, although he confessed he had been badly surprised by the sudden advent of two complete divisions in this particular area, and throughout the interrogation reiterated the*

shattering effect of such immensely superior forces on his already badly depleted troops, which did not number more than 4,000 in all.

General Fiebig had no exact advance information about landing and dropping zones, or times, although he had fully appreciated the likelihood of a landing somewhere in his area. He rather expected the landing farther from the Rhine, in the area east of the River Issel and thought it would take place either at dusk before the land assault or else simultaneously with it.

The Airborne Plan

At the beginning of the planning process, while the Battle of the Rhineland was still in progress, General Sir Miles Dempsey considered it 'absolutely essential to have airborne assistance in crossing the Rhine'. The airborne mission was to be twofold:

(1) *Seize the commanding ground from which artillery fire controlled the whole area.*
(2) *Block possible arrival of enemy reinforcements from Wesel and the east.*

It was decided to drop XVIII US Airborne Corps east of the Rhine after the main 21st Army Group assault across the river. According to Montgomery:

There were two main reasons for this decision: daylight was desirable for the employment of airborne troops and, secondly, it would be impossible to make full use of our artillery for the ground assault if airborne troops were dropped in the target area before we had crossed the river.

When, however, the airborne commanders learnt of General Ridgeway's plans for Operation VARSITY they were shocked at the change of tactics. Gone were the drops deep behind enemy lines, on DZs remote from the enemy and miles from their objectives, in favour of surprise, heavy concentrations of artillery support and true vertical envelopment, by dropping directly on top of the enemy! The whole airborne plan was in effect a vast *coup de main.*

The risks, however, were considerable. An

General Ridgeway.

43

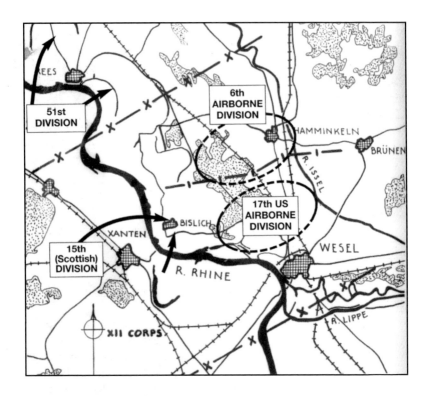

airborne force is at its most vulnerable when landing and to mitigate this, the two divisions of the Corps were to land well concentrated, over a short period of time, after a heavy bombardment, code named CLIMAX. A separate counter-bombardment operation, BLOTTER, was aimed at destroying the enemy artillery. Even though the air forces had finally accepted that the risks to their aircraft in dispatching parachutists and gliders over heavy flak, in order to gain an early advantage, outweighed the cost of struggling to retrieve the situation later, they too demanded mitigating measures. These consisted of an artillery counter flak bombardment (CARPET) as well as the attacks on identified sites by fighter bombers immediately before the drop.

XVIII US Airborne Corps and Plans

General Ridgeway's two divisions earmarked for Operation VARSITY had both been involved in the Battle of the Bulge. 17th US Airborne Division had been training at the time of Market

Garden but were deployed by air on Christmas Day 1944 and marched to take up a defensive position on the Meuse. Later they relieved 28th US Division in the heart of the snow covered Ardennes and fought through the campaign until 10 February, when the division, like 6th Airborne, was withdrawn to prepare for the airborne assault. For a time it was intended to use 82nd Airborne as well but there were insufficient resources to lift three divisions and the 'All Americans' had also been at the heart of the Bulge

XVIII US Airborne Corps' badge.

and it was an easy decision to use just the fresh 17th Airborne Division.

Nicknamed 'Thunder from Heaven', the 17th had been brought up to strength by the transfer of the Normandy veterans of 507 Parachute Infantry Regiment (PIR) from 82nd Airborne. The experienced 507 PIR joined 513 PIR and 194 Glider Infantry Regiment (GIR) who would carry out their first operational drop during VARSITY.

In contrast to MARKET GARDEN where three airborne divisions had been dropped over several days up to sixty miles from the front line, XVIII US Airborne Corps was to land three to seven miles east of the Rhine, in a single daylight lift, with a P-Hour of 1000 hours on D Day (24 March 1945). They were to dislocate the enemy defences, seize vital ground, hold the bridgehead against enemy counter-attacks and capture bridges to facilitate the breakout of 21st Army Group onto the North German Plain. Even though Second Army thought they could possibly do without the airborne assault, in the event of bad weather, the dislocating effect of paratroopers arriving behind the enemy would be decisive in creating the opportunity for XII Corps to develop momentum necessary for a speedy breakout.

In Operation VARSITY, the airborne divisions were not to be committed until a viable bridgehead across the Rhine had been formed by US and British infantry divisions (Operations TURNSCREW, TORCHLIGHT and FLASHLIGHT). In short, the inadequacies and over ambitious planning assumptions of MARKET GARDEN were not to be repeated. It was planned that 15th Scottish Division would link-up with the airborne troops on the first day of the battle and to the south, 30th US Infantry Division would link-up

17th US Airborne Division's badge.

with 17th Airborne. The American Paratroopers were also to be responsible for establishing contact with the Commando Brigade.

The River Issel was about thirty yards wide, with steep banks and was a significant obstacle to armour. Therefore, holding the river-line and crossings was key to both defence against counter-attacks and for facilitating the breakout. The bridges once captured, were to be held but prepared for demolition in case they should fall into the hands of the German XLVII *Panzerkorps*, who would need the bridges to complete their counter-attack against XII Corps's bridgehead between Rees and Wesel.

In the latter stages of the operation, once it had crossed the Rhine, 6 Guards Tank Brigade was to come under command of the Airborne Corps, when the heavy ferries were open. The leading squadron, provided by 3rd Tank Battalion Scots Guards, would be allocated to 6th Airborne Division. The remainder of the Brigade would cross as the development of the battle dictated.

6th Airborne Division's Plan

Major General Eric Bols had taken over command of the division from General Gale, who was now the Deputy Commander of the Airborne Corps. Bols's VARSITY plan for 6th Airborne Division was to drop and land on the northern or left sector in the area in front of XII Corps, with the tasks of seizing the wooded high ground of

the Diesfordterwald, the large village of Hamminkeln and three bridges (code named X, Y and Z) over the River Issel. Linking up with 17th US Airborne Division and forming a defensive northern flank were also important considerations and as soon as heavy ferries were opened, the Scots Guards Churchill tanks would come under command of the British Airborne Division.

In detail, 3 Parachute Brigade was to lead the operation by dropping on DZ A at the north-west corner of the Diesfordterwald, then to clear the forest and seize the Schneppenberg feature at its western edge, overlooking the approach routes to

Major General Eric Bols

be used by XII Corps. In the other side of the forest, the Brigade was to patrol and if necessary hold the area of the railway line which ran through the north-eastern part of the Diesfordterwald.

Meanwhile, on DZ B to the north-west of Hamminkeln, 5

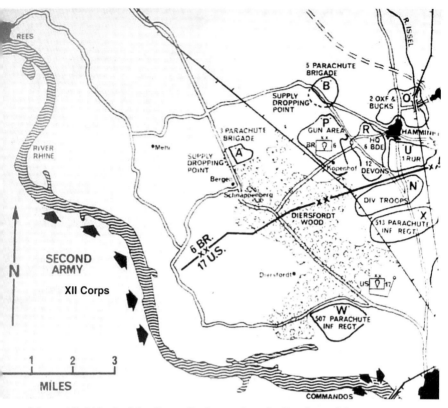

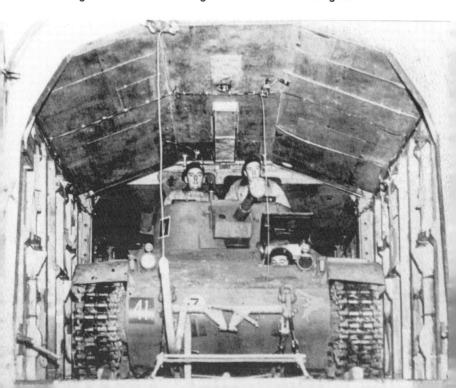

A Locust light tank of the Recce Regiment aboard a Hamilcar glider.

Parachute Brigade would drop, clear and secure the area astride the road from their DZ to Hamminkeln. While dispatching patrols westwards, the bulk of the Brigade was to hold the area to the east of the railway line.

Brigadier Bellamy's 6 Airlanding Brigade, coming in after the two parachute brigades was ordered to land by company groups as close as possible to their objectives, with each battalion being allotted its own Landing Zone. 2 Ox and Bucks Light Infantry (LZ O) and 1 RUR (LZ R) would be responsible for *coup de main* attacks on the three bridges over the River Issel. 12 Devons would land on LZ O and capture Hamminkeln. The intelligence, however, was not reassuring, as air photography revealed that there were numerous flak positions in the area of their glider LZ's.

Following 6 Airlanding Brigade, Divisional HQ and the Airborne Division's artillery group would land by glider in the centre of the divisional area on LZ P. Along with these troops and other essential fly in elements, was C Company of 12 Devons who were to clear and secure the area, as the Division was, after all, landing on its objectives and they could therefore expect opposition across their DZs and LZs.

A divisional reserve was to be formed by two troops totalling eight light Locust tanks from 6 Airborne Armoured Reconnaissance Regiment. These tanks had replaced the Tetrarchs when the division was withdrawn from Normandy in August 1944. They were to fly into LZ P, with one of the 7 ton tanks per Hamilcar glider, and along with guns of the Anti-Tank Regiment, be deployed, as needed, to blunt the expected counter-attacks by XVII *Panzerkorps*.

The Recce Regiment's main tank, the Cromwell, along with its heavy Daimler armoured cars and carriers, left camp to cross the Channel by sea, with the remainder of the Division's Land Tail on 19 March. They masqueraded as 'Stewarts Horse' (after the commanding officer) and their vehicles had their divisional patches and numbers painted out. These vehicles were to be among the first armour across the Rhine, to help the division in its role during the breakout, once the ferries were open.

The organic artillery support of airborne formations was perforce, strictly limited to a single light artillery unit, 53rd (Worcestershire Yeomanry) Airlanding Light Regiment, with its twelve 75mm guns and an attached 4.2-inch mortar troop from the Armoured Recce Regiment. To address the Division's lack of artillery, the guns of XII Corps were to provide support from positions west of the Rhine. The medium and field regiments of 8 Army Group Royal Artillery were on call to XVIII US Airborne Corps as a whole, while the 25-pounder gun group of 52nd Lowland Division, who were out of the line, were in direct support of 6th Airborne Division. Observation officers dropping or landing with the airborne troops would call for fire missions over the radio.

Amphibious Training

While 6th Airborne Division was holding the line of the Maas and enjoying a short period of post operational leave, Second Army was training for the Rhine crossing. Having taken part in the first half of Operation VERITABLE, 15th Scottish Division was selected to lead the assault across the Rhine and were placed under XII Corps on the River Maas for the purposes of developing crossing techniques and for training. Grouped with the Corps was G Wing of 79th Armoured Division ('Hobart's Funnies'), who had already

Amphibious armour, the DD Sherman and the Buffalo Landing vehicle were key elements in the plan to cross the Rhine and hold the resulting bridgehead.

been working on developing or adapting amphibious equipment and tactical doctrine for river crossings. In January, 33 Armoured Brigade joined exchanging their Sherman tanks for the amphibious Buffalo or as it was officially known, the Landing Vehicle Tracked (LVT). The Staffordshire Yeomanry and 44 Royal Tank Regiment under HQ 4 Armoured Brigade also joined the division to retrain with DD tanks. Lieutenant Colonel Hopkinson, Commanding Officer 44 RTR wrote:

> Yes it was all too true, we the 44th Royal Tank Regiment had joined the Wavy Navy and were to sail our way across the Rhine in the same type of DD tanks with inflatable skirts as were used for the amphibious landings on D Day. Then ensued a furious period of training- 10 days – from morning to night. Nautical terms were freely used ...!

Also training on the Maas was 1 Commando Brigade, still under former Guardsman, Brigadier Derek Mills-Roberts, who had taken over command when Lord Lovat was wounded in Normandy. His immediate task was to prepare his men to take the city of Wesel just to the south west of the VARSITY DZs and LZs.

The Brigade commander believed in through training and had his commandos repeat exercises until they were perfect, all the while with the incentive of time off for those who got it right more quickly. Minimizing casualties was also one of his major concerns and he ensured that that his men would not suffer for the want of resources and that casualties would be promptly evacuated. Throughout training, problems were identified, resolved and the mitigating measures were built into the plan.

Preparations

While the British and American paratroopers trained at their respective bases in southern Britain and in France (east of Paris) the Second Army assembled everything that was required for the assault and breakout. Lieutenant Peter White of 4 KOSB, who as part of 52nd (Lowland) Division, holding the area just west of the Rhine, recalled:

> Interesting units and vehicles, including amphibious tanks and Buffaloes, bridging pontoons, hundreds of guns and mountains of ammunition, were piling into every available space. During daylight hours, more and more smoke generators and canisters

A well camouflaged truck brings forward a 40mm Bofors anti-aircraft gun.

tended by pioneers appeared over the countryside, pouring out coiling billows of bluish and yellow smoke screens to keep the enemy guessing on the date and place of the crossing.

A sixty-six mile long smoke screen enveloped the west bank, from Nijmegen south, concealing preparations from observers on the other side of the river. The smoke screen was maintained by four Pioneer Corps smoke companies made up of no less than 1,350

Smoke generation equipment used thousands of gallons of fuel.

men, who one old soldier described as 'ineligible for any other arm of the service, with a sprinkling of intellectuals considered to be of no military value elsewhere'. They worked under a headquarters known as Smoke Control and expended during VERITABLE and PLUNDER 8,500 zinc chloride smoke generators and 450,000 gallons of fog oil in order to maintain the smoke screen. When their work was combined with smoke from the fires in Wesel, it was extremely effective, however, the pilots carrying the airborne divisions into battle, perhaps found their work a little too effective.

If the location of the assault were to remain a secret one thing that had to be controlled was reconnaissance. Lieutenant General Horrocks, commander XXX Corps, explained:

> *Before an attack of this sort a large number of people must go forward and reconnoitre the position they are to occupy. This applies particularly to the Gunners, who have many mysterious rites of their own to perform before they can bring down accurate concentrations of fire. Nobody was allowed forward on to the flat Polderland stretching back from the banks of the Rhine without reporting to a special branch of XXX Corps HQ, where a very large-scale map of the forward area was maintained. This was known as 'The Pig Hotel'. After examining the accommodation on the map which they had been allocated, the reconnaissance parties were allowed to go forward a few at a time to see their 'rooms', which, if satisfactory, were then marked up on the plan as 'booked'.*

General Horrocks highlighted the fact that not every one was as careful as they should have been in the conduct of their recce:

> *I was particularly angry one day to hear that a certain Major General, who was much too brave to take the normal precautions, had walked along the near bank of the Rhine, wearing his red hat. He subsequently left our area, with a monumental flea in his ear.*

To facilitate commanders' daylight recces, the smoke screen was briefly allowed to disperse but on one occasion the wind changed and the commanders peering from camouflaged observation posts built into the dykes only got a 'watery eye squint'.

Potentially, the most obvious preparations were those being made by the Royal Artillery. 1,300 British and 600 US field, medium and heavy guns, their myriad of vehicles and stockpiles of ammunition were hard to conceal. These guns had to be far enough forward, not only to fire in support of the amphibious crossing but the medium artillery was to be in position to provide immediate support to the airborne troops.

So large was the number of guns and so few the routes available for them, it was necessary to bring them up over the nights of 21 to 23 March, using staging areas about six miles from the river. By the morning of 23 March, the majority of the guns were in their forward positions and Captain Whately-Smith wrote:

> As one looked around it was hard to believe that these fields and orchards concealed a mass of artillery waiting in silence for the evening zero hour'.

While Second Army's preparations for the amphibious assault across the Rhine were underway, XVIII US Airborne Corps were similarly making ready at their bases in the UK and France.

Airborne Training

With the plan made, all be it still being refined in detail, and landing tables being prepared by unit air adjutants, the British soldiers and airmen who were to take part in the largest ever airborne operation, undertook task related training packages, culminating in a series of large airborne exercises. Harry Clark a glider infantryman from 2nd Ox and Bucks Light Infantry recalled:

Glider infantry deploying from a Horsa glider during training for Operation VARSITY.

Before this massive operation was launched, a rehearsal for 'Varsity' took place. On the 14 March 1945, Exercise 'Vulture' got under way. Two groups of sixty Dakotas each towed a Mark 2 Horsa glider from RAF Down Ampney. Tasked with flying very big formations, this successful practice gave us an insight into what would take place in just a few days time.

Meanwhile, the two parachute brigades took part in Exercises MUSH I and II in the Bury St Edmunds area of East Anglia, which were in fact the final rehearsal for VARSITY.

Amongst the members of the Glider Pilot Regiment (GPR) there were a few crews who had taken part in the Sicily, Normandy and Arnhem operations and survived to tell the tale. However, flying many of the gliders were RAF aircrew. So heavy had the casualties been amongst the Glider Pilot Regiment at Arnhem, only 700 were available to meet VARSITY's requirement for up to 2,000 pilots.

The RAF, with a surplus of pilots following a significant drop in Bomber Command casualties, once British and Canadian night fighters were able to operate with the bombers, was well placed to make good this deficiency. In the immediate aftermath of MARKET GARDEN they had set about training selected men from their thousands of surplus aircrew as glider pilots. As Stan Jarvis, who had been taught to fly at Falcon Field in the USA, said 'it was necessary to borrow a number of RAF pilots, of whom I was one, to fly the military gliders across the Rhine'. Warrant Officer Len Macdonald recalled that he had completed training in Oklahoma, when:

Stan Jarvis trained RAF pilot and 'volunteer' glider pilot.

… in October 1944 I found myself in the company of some 200 RAF pilots on parade at 0830 hours on the car park of the Majestic Hotel in Harrogate. Roll-call completed we were addressed by the officer in charge of the parade (who must for the sake of his personal safety remain nameless). 'You lot', he said, 'You lot have just volunteered to fly gliders'. He said this with a certain amount of relish, happy at being shot of, at a single

A company commander with maps and air photography briefs his men.

stroke, some 200 bods who neither he nor the RAF quite knew how to gainfully employ at that time.

The flying training was relatively straightforward for men who were already trained pilots, except they had '…to learn that they could not simply throttle up to get out of trouble'. Len Macdonald continued:

Apart from the odd run-march and a night march armed only with a compass, with the rendezvous at some God-forsaken pub in Berkshire very little time was spent on trying to turn me into a soldier...The importance of DCOSF (Down, crawl, observe, sight, fire) [reaction to effective enemy fire] was heavily underlined.

Other pressed glider pilots were taken in hand by their Glider Pilot Regiment partners, with whom RAF pilots were normally paired, and taken on the range to fire their Sten guns. They were also introduced to unfamiliar field equipment and most of them listened avidly to the war stories of Sicily, Normandy and Arnhem told by their Army comrades in the NAAFI canteen. Consequently, despite the brevity of their training, they were imbued with the ethos of the GPR and understood their role and what was expected of them in the coming battle. A measure of their success is afforded by contrasting the esteem that their USAAF counterparts were held; few American airborne soldiers had anything good to say about their glider pilots once on the ground. On the other hand, the RAF glider pilots are universally considered to have earned their red berets in battle. There can be no higher praise than this.

Final Preparations

With training and exercises completed, 6th Airborne Division was moved to sealed camps for detailed briefing. The Division left its camps at Bulford and Larkhill on Salisbury Plain by circuitous route (for security reasons) at 0600 hours on 18 March. They arrived at their RAF transit camp at 1630 hours. One member of 12 Devons commented that Gosfield Camp in Essex was 'Very badly arranged, with a twenty minute walk for meals and very inadequate messes'. Virtually all soldiers' accounts of this period describe the food in these camps as being what can only be politely described as 'execrable', even by wartime standards. The day after arrival, the Battalion was able to stretch its legs with an eight mile march and run after breakfast before settling down to loading their aircraft.

Corporal Cooper of the Airlanding Field Ambulance wrote:

Sten g
and
magaz
Standa
issue
glider
pilots.

21 ARMY GROUP

PERSONAL MESSAGE
FROM THE C-IN-C

(To be read out to all Troops)

1. On the 7th February I told you we were going into the ring for the final and last round; there would be no time limit: we would continue fighting until our opponent was knocked out. The last round is going very well on both sides of the ring—and overhead.

2. In the WEST, the enemy has lost the Rhineland, and with it the flower of at least four armies—the Parachute Army, Fifth Panzer Army, Fifteenth Army, and Seventh Army; the First Army, further to the south, is now being added to the list.

   In the Rhineland battles, the enemy has lost about 150,000 prisoners, and there are many more to come; his total casualties amount to about 250,000 since 8th February.

3. In the EAST, the enemy has lost all POMERANIA east of the ODER, an area as large as the Rhineland; and three more German armies have been routed. The Russian armies are within about 35 miles of BERLIN.

4. Overhead, the Allied Air Forces are pounding Germany day and night. It will be interesting to see how much longer the Germans can stand it.

5. The enemy has in fact been driven into a corner, and he cannot escape.

   Events are moving rapidly.

   The complete and decisive defeat of the Germans is certain; there is no possibility of doubt on this matter.

6. 21 ARMY GROUP WILL NOW CROSS THE RHINE.

   The enemy possibly thinks he is safe behind this great river obstacle. We all agree that it is a great obstacle; but we will show the enemy that he is far from safe behind it. This great Allied fighting machine, composed of integrated land and air forces, will deal with the problem in no uncertain manner.

7. And having crossed the RHINE, we will crack about in the plains of Northern Germany, chasing the enemy from pillar to post. The swifter and the more energetic our action the sooner the war will be over, and that is what we all desire: to get on with the job and finish off the German war as soon as possible.

8. Over the RHINE, then, let us go. And good hunting to you all on the other side.

9. May "the Lord mighty in battle" give us the victory in this our latest undertaking, as He has done in all our battles since we landed in Normandy on D-day.

B. L. Montgomery

Field-Marshal,
C.-in-C.,
21 Army Group.

Germany,
March, 1945.

On the 20th March, we were moved to a transit camp, as part of the US Airborne Corps. Here we were kept busy making up payloads for the gliders. The maximum load for a Horsa glider was 6,000 lbs; each glider carried 24 men or a jeep and 15 men or a jeep with a trailer and 6 men. The average weight of a man and his personal equipment was 210 lbs, and the weight of every piece of extra equipment had to be determined. A great deal of juggling was entailed so that eventually the contents of each glider were as near as possible to the maximum payload, without exceeding it. The glider that I was to travel in carried a jeep and 15 men. The jeep occupied the centre of the glider with 9 men at the front and 6 men at the rear of the glider, the jeep effectively cutting off communication between the two parties.

Security surrounding the operation was tight and the camps and airfields were sealed in order to prevent word of the coming operation leaking. On 23 March, all officers and NCO's were called to briefings, which were very thorough. Unlike during the run-up to Arnhem, every piece of information was analysed and every contingency considered by commanders from General Bols downwards. Corporal Cooper recalled some of the detail that was passed down to him

Aerial photographs of the area of the landing zones were shown to us as these were in 3D [stereo pairs] we got a very good idea of the terrain and were actually able to pick a point at which to assemble after landing, from where we would proceed to the building which had been chosen as a suitable for the Main Dressing Station. We were also advised that along the base of our triangular landing zone were high-tension power lines, and the glider pilots were warned not to come too low although there was no current passing along the cables as the RAF had bombed the power station.

Lieutenant Allanson, a platoon commander in B Company 12 Devon recalls that his briefing was equally thorough: 'Major Wally Barrow then briefed the officers and sergeants of the Company in every detail from maps, photographs and a model. This took nearly three hours and all felt extremely tired ...' After tea Lieutenant Allanson got his 'own stuff together and wondered how I was going to carry it all'.

Corporal Cooper recalled the final pep talks.

We were also told that aerial observation had seen no heavy artillery in the area and the operation was regarded as 'A piece of cake.' Indeed, General Montgomery, we were told, had expressed the view that he did not think that we were really necessary but that we were thrown in as a makeweight, - Not exactly morale raising.

Brigadier James Hill, Commander 3 Parachute Brigade was more positive in the final section of his briefing to 1st Canadian Para Battalion:

Gentlemen, the artillery and air support is fantastic! And if you

Brigadier James Hill talking to officers of 1st Canadians Para battalions at the end of his MUSH Exercise.

are worried about the kind of reception you'll get, just put yourself in the place of the enemy. Beaten and demoralised, pounded by our artillery and bombers, what would you think, gentlemen, if you saw a horde of ferocious, bloodthirsty paratroopers, bristling with weapons, cascading down upon you from the skies? And you needn't think, just because you hear a few stray bullets flying about, that some miserable Hun is shooting at you. That is merely a form of egotism. But if by any chance you should happen to meet one of these Huns in person, you will treat him, gentlemen, with extreme disfavour.

6th Airborne Division was briefed that neither the politicians nor the public would stand for another Arnhem and they were told that the operation could be cancelled right up to the moment of the drop if Second Army had not already established firm bridgeheads and was in a position to guarantee a prompt link up.

All was ready but 12 Devon's historian described an 'air of unreality' that pervaded their transit camp during the final hours before take off, with men going to bed about 2200 hours to try and 'avoid that sinking feeling' that grows in a sleepless night before an operation.

CHAPTER FOUR

The Amphibious Operations

(For full details see Battleground PLUNDER)

Unlike Operations HUSKY, OVERLORD and MARKET GARDEN, which all opened with airborne operations, PLUNDER, the Rhine Crossing, was to begin with the amphibious assault in order to establish a viable bridgehead before XVIII US Airborne Corps would begin its drop.

The air bombing and artillery bombardment by the prodigious number of guns assembled to support the operation started to grow from 1700 hours on 23 March 1945. This was the beginning of what was the greatest British artillery bombardment of the war, being fire by some 5,500 guns. Major Martin Lindsay of 1 Gordons, recalled that:

There was a continuous ripple of slams and bangs as all our guns, stretching across so many fields behind, were firing, and it went on for four hours … Meanwhile quite a lot of stuff was beginning to come back from the other side, mostly medium and light mortars. One mortar in particular was dropping its bombs all round this house. At 7.30 p.m., there was still one and a half hours to go. A tremendous rumble of guns behind us, their shells whistling overhead, and the nice sharp banging sound of our 25-pounders landing on the far bank.

Operation TURNSCREW

In typical Montgomery style, the Rhine Crossing began with an attack designed to widen the frontage of the assault, focus the enemy's attention away from the site of his main effort and to get enemy reserves heading away from where they would be most required. To this end, XXX Corps launched 51st Highland Division, in Operation TURNSCREW astride the riverside town of Rees ten miles north of the point where XII Corps (the main effort) would cross.

In flickering light of the bombardment, at 2030 hours, as described in Second Army's history, the 51st Division's:

'… assault formations slipped out of their hides and turned their

61

Landing Vehicle Tracked (LVT) more commonly known in British Service as the Buffalo.

LVTs towards the east. Across the broad floodplain toward the dark swift-running waters of the great barrier of the R Rhine amphibians picked their careful paths, assisted by movement light. A tremendous artillery barrage roared encouragement. The curtain had risen on the opening phases of the last battle of the European war'.

As any force forming up on the riverbank would be detected by the enemy, the initial assault troops were all mounted in LVTs (Buffalos) and, with the DD tanks of the Staffordshire Yeomanry following, they motored down from their hides, on pre-recced routes, to the crossing points. The bombardment covered the noise of the track, while softening up the 8th *Fallschirmjäger* Division, dug-in on the far bank. Several artillery regiments engaged the landing areas on the far bank with the aim of detonating enemy landmines.

The four leading battalions from the two assault brigades, 153 and 154, were mounted in 150 amphibious Buffalos, with one troop of four LVTs being allocated per infantry company. Their tasks were to secure the bank and objectives little more than a thousand yards inland. In the case of 153 Brigade, their second wave (1 Gordon) was to capture Rees, while that of 154 Brigade (1 Black Watch) was to expand the bridgehead by capturing the villages of Speldrop and Klein Esserden. 152 Brigade was to send a battalion (2nd Seaforth) over the river to support 153 Brigade in the capture of Rees before midnight on D-1. The remainder of the Division were to follow and further expand the bridgehead.

Trooper Walter Fuller of 4 RTR, carrying 153 Brigade, recalled:

For this operation our Shermans had been replaced with American Buffalo amphibious tanks [LVT personnel carriers], supporting the 51st Highland Division. It was pitch black as we led our vehicles into the water, we couldn't see and had no idea what to expect, other than that being the first unit over the Rhine no doubt meant resistance would be heavy. It was an extremely nerve-wracking crossing, especially as we had only just changed over from the Shermans we were used to! After a while though we realised that in fact there was next to no resistance and our

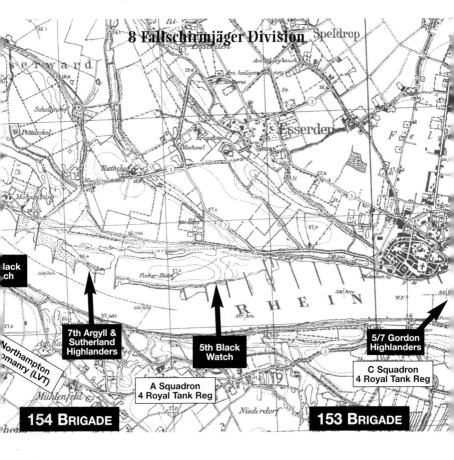

Buffalos on the Rhine on the Operation PLUNDER D-Day.

*crossing was all but uncontested, which was a huge relief. When
we reached the other side I remember one man, Colonel Alan Jolly
[CO 4 RTR], planting the regimental flag on the eastern bank of
the river. It was in fact the very same flag taken into battle by the
unit in the First World War and was a proud moment for us all.*

Highland infantryman Bill Robertson crossing with the first wave
of 154 Brigade recalled that things looked difficult for a time.

*My most vivid memory of WWII was crossing the Rhine …1945;
four days after my 19th birthday … in amphibious vehicles called
buffalos with were run by the Northamptonshire Yeomanry. We
were halfway across when our tracks locked and we went around
in a circle and drifted. We all thought we were going to have to
jump or swim for it, but at the last minute the tracks started up
again.*

Commander XXX Corps, General Horrocks, in an observation post
on some high ground overlooking the Rhine, recalled that 'All
around me were the usual noises of battle but I could see very little
except the flicker of the guns'. Horrocks, however, soon received a
message, at 2117 hours; 'The Black Watch has landed safely on the
far bank'.

The task given to 154 Brigade was to form a bridgehead a mile
and a half deep, to the east of Rees, including the villages of Kline
Esserden and Speldrop. The assault was to be led by 7 Black Watch
and 7 Argyles, with the third battalion, 1 Black Watch, crossing into
the bridgehead later.

The leading battalions climbed up the steep banks, out of the
river in their tracked amphibians with a little difficulty, astride
Mahnenburg. One of the Northamptonshire Yeomanry's LVT was
knocked out by a *Teller-mine*, on the enemy bank. While 7 Black
Watch were debusing from their Buffalos, further casualties were
sustained from anti-personnel *Schumines* that had been scattered
thinly along the banks. Accompanying the infantry were engineers
of 274 Field Company, whose task was to clear the bank of mines
before the arrival of the subsequent waves, as well as helping
construct exit ramps to ease their passage. Enemy opposition was
minimal to start with; the *Fallschirmjäger* defenders were still
stunned by the effect of the bombardment. However, moving
inland, resistance stiffened and fighting around the villages of
Kline Esserden and Speldrop went on for much of the day, with
repeated attack and counter-attack.

The light airborne bulldozer carried across the Rhine in a LVT proved its worth on the enemy bank.

153 Brigade's attack astride Rees, on the Divisions right, went equally well but also faced challenges as they advanced from the immediate area of the river bank. They had benefited from the British barrage, which:

> ... had been murderously heavy; it had included salvos of rockets fired from tanks; much of the kick had been taken out of the defence. The first companies passed over many positions whose garrisons were still dazed; as the succeeding companies reached them they were just coming to life.

5 Black Watch cleared Esserden, while 5/7 Gordons, to the south east of Rees landed on an island created by the old course of the Rhine. 1 Gordon Highlanders, following in assault boats, landed between the two leading battalions and headed towards the town of Rees, which was the divisional main effort. The town was, however, not taken for another thirty-six hours. Meanwhile, to complete the isolation of Rees, 152 Brigade crossed the river and 2 Seaforth established itself north of the town against growing opposition.

See map page 63

The first phase of Operation PLUNDER had got underway successfully but it was already apparent that the Germans were going to fight for every inch and their armoured reserves had not yet arrived.

DD Tanks

Meanwhile, two squadrons of DD tanks of the Staffordshire Yeomanry had started crossing the river behind and between the two infantry brigades. They were responsible for making their own exits and on the far bank, they took a considerable amount of time and, in many cases, the tanks found the designated exits impossible. However, crossing in one of the Yeomanry's six Buffalos was an airborne bulldozer, which once ashore, was able to reduce the bank to a slope and several carpets made of coir matting, stiffened with scaffolding poles, were laid to provide a firm surface. With the exits made, the tanks could cross. Lieutenant Sadler continued:

> *I was first tank into the River. We went down the slope, on the way we had quite a bit of gunfire and one or two of the tanks had their canvas screens holed so they couldn't do the trip.*
>
> *We got into the river, which was quite fast flowing. I seemed to have been there a long time and I didn't see the two green lights, but suddenly I saw one green light. I thought, well, the other one might have gone out or something, so I started to land and I found out I was on a mud bank. Before I realized where I was (I thought I'd crossed the river), I let the canvas side down and of course my other two tanks, or three in actual fact, came over and one got stuck in the mud. There was a shellfire going on at that time. It was very uncomfortable and I had to get out of the tank, get the chains out and hook on to the other tank and pull it out. Of course, then I had the problem of whether to risk going from the mud bank to the actual true bank of the river. I probably didn't have enough air anyway to inflate the screen again, … as it happened, the water didn't come up above turret level so we were all right. The other three tanks followed.*

The difficulty in locating the DD exit point was due to the fact that it was not directly or even obliquely across the river but almost a mile down stream. The 3 knot current swept the ungainly and barely 'seaworthy' tanks down stream through the 154 Brigade LVT

DD Shermans making their way to the Rhine.

crossing loop.

By 0600 hours two troops of the Staffordshire Yeomanry's DD tanks were across and ready for action. With the laying of the coir carpets further out into the river and daylight, the speed of crossing increased markedly and the first squadron was supporting the infantry at 0700 hours. The DD Shermans had been used to help solve the perennial problem of assault crossings of major waterways; being able to get tanks across in time to defeat enemy counter-attacks. The remaining two squadrons would, however not be able to cross until the Royal Engineers opened their Class 50/60 ferries.

Operation Widgeon

Under command of XII Corps, 1 Commando Brigade was to conduct another important preliminary assault crossing of the Rhine an hour after the initial assault by 51st Highland Division. They were given the task of seizing the city of Wesel, an important communications centre on the east bank, which was also an enemy strongpoint that, if not captured promptly, would dominate important crossing points and routes in the centre of 21st Army Group's area of operations. Lieutenant General Ritchie, Commander XII Corps:

> ... had given it as his considered opinion that the whole of the operation as it affected his formation depended on this assault being successful. It was considered too, that the success of the attack on the town depended in turn largely on the success of two very heavy bombing raids on the area.

At Wesel, the Rhine was narrower than elsewhere; at about two hundred yards wide but the speed through the restricted channel was around five knots. The river was prevented from flooding by dykes, from fifteen to twenty feet in height. While the town was built on the banks of the river behind high dykes, to the north-west there was several hundred yards of open flood plain. Wesel itself was a medium size town of some twenty-four thousand inhabitants and strongly built, largely of stone, with a high proportion of wood. Like most towns on the Rhine, Wesel had already been bombed by the Allies, finally by seventy-seven Lancasters of No. 3 Group on the afternoon before the attack.

Armed Hitlerjugend were used in the front line across the Varsity and Plunder area.

There was not much information on the enemy in the town, which was in the sector thought to be held by *General Major* Heinz Fiebig's 84th *Volksgreandier* Division. At least one of the numerous *erzats* battalions (probably 317th), made up of administrative troops extracted from the rear area had been identified in Wesel. Later, a two star German command post belonging to the garrison commander was also found within the town.

1 Commando Brigade was 'to seize Wesel and the bridges over the Lippe to the south of it, and hold the eastern and southern exits of the town'. Brigadier Mills-Roberts's plan was based on five factors: first, that to take advantage of the bombing raids they were to cross the river before the second raid and be 'ready to rush into the city while its defences were still 'punch drunk'; secondly, to achieve surprise, it was decided to cross at an unlikely spot, a muddy flood plain two miles west of Wesel; thirdly, there was to be no attempt to secure the entire town, as it would not be possible to clear it, before the enemy counter-attacks; the Brigade would therefore seize a factory area dominating the northern edge of Wesel; fourthly, there should be no trace of the Brigade on the flood plain at dawn, leaving the Germans unaware of their strength and whereabouts. Fifthly, landing across the muddy flood plain they would be unable to take heavy weapons.

The four commando units, 45 and 46 Commandos Royal

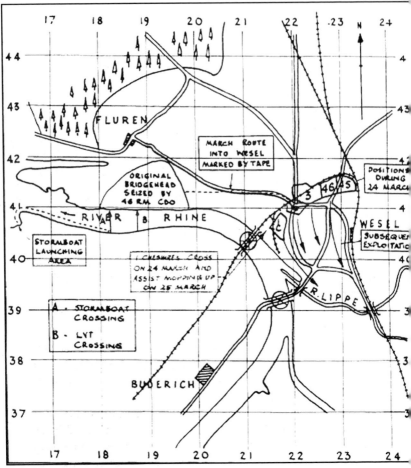

1 Commando Brigade's Operation WIDGEON Plan.

Marines and Nos. 3 and 6 (Army) Commandos, were joined by 84 Field Company RE and forward observation parties from 1st Mountain Regiment RA, who would call for artillery fire. Sufficient LVTs were allocated to carry a single commando across the river in one lift, before returning to collect subsequent waves.

At 2200 hours, H Hour for Operation WIDGEON, 6 Field Regiment's shells, being fired at a rapid rate for the ten minutes of the initial crossing, were bursting on the bank opposite, drowning out the sound of everything else. Suddenly the area was lit up by fifteen foot flames from a direct hit on one of the Buffaloes on the far bank. 'This beacon like blaze attracted the Germans attention and brought more shells and mortar bombs'.

Clearing a bridgehead took just fifteen minutes against some resistance and 46 RM Commando were soon waiting for the RAF raid on Wesel. BBC correspondent Stewart Macpherson was watching the crossing from the home bank and recorded the following:

I watched the [last] commandos take off for Wesel … A few minutes after they were due to arrive on the far side, bomber command were to deliver a crushing blow on the enemy in Wesel, while the commandos lay doggo over there, a bare thousand yards from the bomber target, and waited. Smack on time, Arthur Harris & Company, House Removers, as they were called by the commandos, arrived and delivered a nerve-shaking blow on the former Wesel stronghold. Back at Headquarters, minutes ticked by. Officers waited anxiously for word from the commandos across the river. Suddenly there was a signal, and a voice literally purred over the wireless: 'Noisy blighters, aren't they?'

The 'noisy blighters', 201 RAF heavy bombers, had arrived at 2230 hours and dropped 1,100 tons of bombs. The Army had in fact requested a raid of only 300 tons of high explosive but as usual the RAF had increased the tonnage.

Leading off with a tape laying party No. 6 Commando headed for Wesel and entered the city, with the remainder of the Brigade following through a bomb damaged archway formed of hideously buckled rails and sleepers. Once in the city the ground changed totally. One commando described the scene that greeted them:

The streets were unrecognisable and many of the buildings were mere mounds of rubble. Huge craters abounded and into these flowed water mains and sewers, accompanied by escapes of flaming gas. We were held up in one street because the two leading scouts found great difficulty in making their way round between a crater and one of the buildings. It took some minutes before a better route was found further to the right. The scene was well illuminated for the ensuing battle in the streets by the many fires that blazed on all sides. Despite the heavy bombing the Germans were alert and came out of the cellars to fight with a courage and perseverance which did them great credit. The air was full of smoke and dust which was like breathing a particularly nauseous fog.

The Rhine to the east of Wesel in the Widgeon Area.

Rather than attempt to clear the city the commandos headed to pre-selected positions on the northern edge of built up area. With the last commando in place by 0200 hours, the men laboured to prepare defences to meet the expected counter-attacks. Meanwhile, to dominate the ground and to gather information, patrols probed back into the city. The result of one of these patrols was recorded by the Brigade Commander:

> Generalmajor *Deutch, the German Garrison Commander, was found by a patrol of 6 Commando in his headquarters in a cellar. He refused to surrender and was killed by a burst of Tommy gun fire. In his headquarters was a map giving full details of the flak dispositions of the whole area. It was invaluable because next day the 18th Airborne Corps, American and British, was to fly in and before that time it would be possible to get our own artillery on to the German flak positions to hammer them and do as much damage as possible.*

At dawn the German counter-attacks began and built as leading elements of XLVII *Panzerkorps* started to arrive. The most dangerous period for the Commando Brigade was between 1000 hours and 1300 hours, during the fly-in, as artillery firing on the approaches to Wesel was subject to a check-fire. As expected, this coincided with them coming under severe pressure from 115th Panzer Division and some question the decision to not take anti-tank guns with the commando units; instead relying on captured *panzerfausts*.

Operation TORCHLIGHT

The Second Army's Operation PLUNDER main effort lay with XII Corps who were to lead their assault across the Rhine with 15th Scottish Division, who had, as has been explained, been extracted from VERITABLE, after the initial phases, to train and prepare for PLUNDER.

XII Corps's task was, with or without the drop of XVIII US Airborne Corps, to force a crossing of the Rhine, seize the Issel bridges (if not captured by 6th Airborne), establish ferries and eventually bridge the Rhine. From the resulting bridgehead, the Corps was to be prepared to operate eastwards. To this end, a Mobile Striking Force based on an armoured regiment and an infantry battalion mounted in Kangaroo armoured personnel carriers, was to be given the highest priority on the ferries and was to be ready for operations by first light on D plus 2.

15th (Scottish) Division was to launch its assault at 0200 hours on 24 March, some five hours after the attack by 51st Highland Division and four hours after that of 1 Commando Brigade. The crossing was timed to be coordinated with that of the crossing of XVI US Corps to their south (Operation FLASHLIGHT).

Enemy Forces

XII Corps, although they were unsure of the exact enemy boundaries, knew that their assault area was opposite elements of 7th *Fallschirmjäger* Division and 84th Infantry Division, both of which, as already discussed were shadows of their former selves. However, in prepared positions they were still expected to give a good account of themselves against the vulnerable Scottish infantry advancing across the river and open flood plain. It was known that the defenders in the 84th Division area now included *Volkststurm* but these reinforcements, on the face of it, of very low quality but similar troops had given a good account of themselves during the battle of the Bulge and of course during VERITABLE, when they had already faced 15th Scottish Division.

An estimate of the quantity of enemy artillery that XII Corps would face was made by gunner intelligence:

> '... 84th Inf Div assisted by GHQ and non-divisional resources, was thought to have only about fifty medium guns: in fact there were probably more, and they were in any case very difficult to locate, as they were mostly sited in very enclosed country. To this

79th Armoured Division's CDL tanks join Monty's Moonlight Operations.

figure must be added the guns which 7 Para Div might bring to bear against 12 Corps.'

This total did not include the more manoeuvrable and even more difficult to locate, medium mortars, which, throughout the North West European Campaign, was the weapon system that inflicted the greatest proportion of casualties amongst the Allies.

15th Division's Plan

Major General Barber's task was, on a two brigade frontage, to establish a bridgehead between Bislich and Vynen, 'preparatory to securing the area of Bergerfurth along with its bridge', which is referred to as 'Bridge A'. This bridge was important, as the old course of the Rhine was, in effect, a second obstacle or potential line of resistance to be crossed before the Scots could relieve 6th Airborne Division in the area of Hamminkeln. If not already

secured, 15th Division was to go on and capture the bridges over the Issel. No less than six field regiments four or five medium regiments one or two heavy AA batteries and a pair of heavy and super heavy batteries would support each of the assault brigades. The crushing weight of fire delivered by these guns would be supplemented by those of the remainder of 8 Army Group Royal Artillery in the case of emergency. The apogee of the British artillery's power was the 'Pepper Pot'. These bombardments included all available guns being concentrated in an annihilating strike against specific targets and were built into the general fire plan to maximise effect on important targets.

A key part of Major General Barber's plan included 100 Anti-Aircraft Brigade. In addition to its normal role of protecting the ferry and bridging sites from enemy aircraft, this brigade was also to provide river security by coordinating the efforts to prevent the Germans from destroying the crossing sites and bridges with mines laid by divers swimming down stream.

44 Lowland Brigade – Codeword POKER

On 15th Division's right flank the Lowland Brigade was to cross the Rhine and capture and hold the area Schuttwick, Loh and Bislich. 11 RTR (LVT) were to lift the assault battalions of 44 Brigade, 6 Royal Scots Fusiliers (6 RSF) were right assault and 8 Royal Scots (8 RS) left. Their initial objectives were to clear the line of the bund immediately west of Bislich, between Fahrhaus and Ronduit and to occupy the western half of Bislich. Thereafter, 6 King's Own Scottish Boarders (6 KOSB)'was then to pass through 6 RSF and seize the remainder of Bislich, after which the whole brigade was to advance between north and east to the Dieserfordterwald where it was anticipated they would link up with the British and American airborne Troops.

Infantry crossing the home bank's bund during the morning of 24 March.

Staffordshire Yeomanry's DD tanks on the morning of 24 March, ready to support the Jocks.

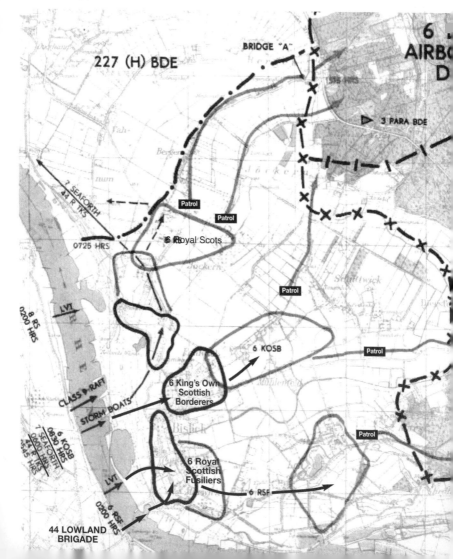

Having received word of the success of the crossing by 51st Highland Division to their north and the Commandos just to their east, 'soon after midnight 23/24 March, the assaulting battalions boarded their LVTs in the Marshalling Area.' Under the cover of the sound of fighting to the flanks and their own "Pepperpot" barrage falling on the opposite bank, the two regiments of Buffaloes each set out for the river, in a single file, at 0330 hours. By 0155 hours … waves of tightly packed Buffaloes roared and squeaked their way through gaps blown by the REs in the dyke wall to splash towards their objectives.' Here 'the columns paused momentarily … to check timings', and then the first flights, comprising three companies per assaulting battalion, passed through the gaps, fanned out into line and entered the water at H Hour (0200 hours).

The Buffalos, having been carried down stream to the approximate area of their proposed landing, headed for the bank and started to climb out of the river. At this point, it was intended that the soldiers of 6 RSF would be led into battle by a battalion piper. BBC radio reporter Wynford Vaughan Thomas was aboard an LVT with the Commanding Officer who:

> … gave the signal, the piper lifted his pipes to his lips, and he blew, and only an agonised wailing came from his instrument. Again he tried, and again the wail. If ever a man was near to tears, it was our piper. His great moment, and now, as he cried in despair: "Ma pipes, man, they'll no play."

Battalion records, however, differ and show that Piper McGhee played the regiment march Cutty's Wedding. He recalled 'There was nothing to do it, but I was a bit scared when I first boarded the Buffalo. There was a good deal of sniping and mortar fire, but the actual crossing wasn't too bad.'

The leading battalions were all across on time, around dawn, having been disembarked 'dry shod'. There was some shelling and mortaring and both 6 RSF and 8 RS reported 'a certain amount of trouble from light automatic fire'. Casualties from anti-personnel mines around the landing sites, drop shorts from their own artillery and the few determined enemy machine gun posts, were overcome with considerable dash. The Jocks occupied the western outskirts of Bislich and Gossenhof Farm, which was captured after a sharp fight with the enemy who were all killed or captured.

By 0330 hours, the Brigade's initial objectives were taken, 'though mopping up was still continuing, some enemy parties

A Buffalo climbs the steep river bank.

having gone to ground in cellars'. As a result, 'patrols were sent out to clean up any enemy who might be lying up in houses or entrenched in their respective areas'.

When the message came through to HQ 44 Brigade that the leading assault companies were established, Brigadier Cumming-Bruce ordered his reserve battalion, 6 KOSB to cross the river by boat. At 0330 hours, two Companies started crossing and, suffered the usual breakdowns of the unreliable storm boat engines. Eighteen year old Private Frederick Hambly recalled his trip across the river:

See map page 76

> *The noise of the battle raging overhead was terrific as we approached the area of embarkation. We, D Company, 6th Bn KOSB embarked on our frail craft, cast off from the west bank. We were nearly halfway across when the engine cut out. We watched as our landing area on the far bank, with its white tapes denoting that that area has been cleared of mines, receded from us, as being without engine power we were swept by the strong current, broadside towards the North Sea!*
>
> *We were however fortunate enough to be spotted by another boat returning for its second run, and its skipper manoeuvred around the stern to our port side, lashed the two boats together and steadily moved upstream to our disembarkation area.*

Having formed up and crossed the flood plain, the second wave of the Borderers cleared the north east part of Bislich and Feldwick. Here they met some resistance from Grenadier Regiment 1062 but by 0700 hours, they were secure in the village.

Once the KOSB were in their position, 44 Lowland Brigade had a continuous bridgehead and were ready to push forward towards the Deiserfordterwald where, just beyond, in a matter of hours, 6th Airborne would be dropping.

227 Highland Brigade – Codeword NAP

The Highland Brigade was to cross the Rhine, capture and hold the area of Haffen and Mehr. Brigadier Colville's plan was to assault with two battalions up, 10 Highland Light Infantry (10 HLI) on the right and 2 Argyll and Sutherland Highlanders (2 A&SH) to the left. 2 Gordon, initially in reserve, and was to cross on orders, when Overkamp and Lohr were reported clear, relieving 10 HLI and 2 A&SH respectively: the latter battalions were then to exploit to Bellinguoven and Wisshof. Once established in their bridgeheads, the two assault brigades would close the gap between them, up to their mutual boundary, while 227 Brigade would be responsible for linking up with 51st Highland Division near Rees.

227 Highland Brigade's crossing of, however, did not go nearly as well as that of 44 Brigade. The leading companies of 10 HLI crossed without casualties, but were landed several hundred yards to the right, missing their objective of Wolffskath, opening a wide gap between the two assault battalions. The HLI found the bund strongly held by three companies of 1/21 *Fallschirmjäger* Regiment, with a strongpoint at Wolffsrath. A Company suffered heavy casualties, including all their officers.

The second flight also landed incorrectly, resulting in 'a highly confused situation', not helped by the absence of Battalion HQ, which had landed to the right and was temporarily stranded in no-man's-land, where it was attacked and 'only extricated at 0500 hours with some difficulty'. That 'difficulty' included '…the complete O.P. party of the 131st Field Regiment, R.A., being ambushed and wiped out'. However, with the guns of the artillery finally answering the call for fire:

> Down came the concentration exactly where it was wanted, whereupon C and D Companies - totalling together much less than one company's strength -went in, in open order. They took Bettenhof together with forty-four prisoners, and there in the southern portion of Overkamp they dug in.

By dawn, 10 HLI were secure in the outskirts of Overkamp, where they were joined by Support Company and essential vehicles

Crossing at the same time, 2nd Argyles had considerable difficulty in getting their Buffaloes ashore thanks to mud banks obstructing the proposed exits from the river. As a result, five out of D Company's six Buffaloes, found it impossible to land at the eastern corner of the inlet as planned, so they climbed ashore on the west side. 'Thus D Company had a mile's march round the inlet before they could tackle Hübsch, so all hope of surprise was lost'. Consequently, outside Hübsch they were engaged in close quarter fighting with *Fallschirmjäger*, who were positioned on the reverse side of the bund and in scrub to the southward. By first light, however, the Argyle's cleared Hübsch, losing many men in the process.

Meanwhile, on the Argyle's left, B and A Companies who landed without casualties, had pushed north without waiting for Hübsch to be cleared and took Hoverhof, north-west of Haffen. Also seen off, was a two-company *Fallschirmjäger* counter-attack with the help of artillery fire.

Pushing north against enemy positions held by *Fallschirmjäger*, the Argyles closed up to the right flank of 51st Highland Division (5/7 Gordons). The actual linkup was not, however, made until P.M. 26 March.

At 0615 hours, 227 Brigade's reserve battalion, 2 Gordons, were ordered to send a company across the river in storm boats. A Company, who were expecting orders for a direct crossing, now found themselves cruising a mile down stream to to join the Argyles. In doing so, they suffered fourteen casualties from small arms fire from isolated enemy posts along the riverbank. B Company were mortared very badly in their assembly area and with the loss of boats, temporarily abandoned their attempt to cross. The presence of these isolated posts caused a significant delay in 15th Scottish Division's build up during the morning of 24 March.

Further advances east were made by the Argyles towards Lohr and Riswickhof but by the time the attack got going, the artillery check fire had been imposed, while air strikes prior to the airborne operation were launched. 1 Middlesex's medium machine guns, however, were available in quantity. The enemy put up significant resistance and it was slow going for the Scots infantry it wasn't until 1330 hours that Lohr, five hundred yards further on, was clear.

Meanwhile, starting at 1030 hours, the remainder of 2 Gordons

Fallschirmjäger machine gunners await the enemy.

Scottish infantry in one of the riverside towns.

A Scottish infantryman provides covering fire with his No 4 Enfield rifle from well inside a room, thus avoiding being framed in the window.

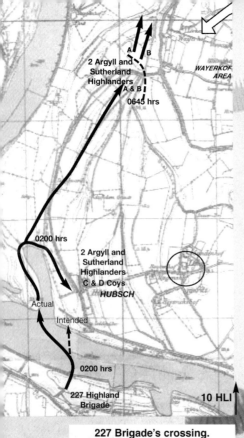

227 Brigade's crossing.

crossed the river. Their historian wrote:

... the Battalion crossed to reinforce the Argylls. There were some minor troubles. The boat conveying the commanding officer and the adjutant ran out of petrol in mid-stream and was paddled until the sapper in charge produced a reserve tin.

Their task was to follow elements of the Argyles around the left flank to attack Haffen and secure the eastern part of Area X. This area in the centre of the 'Bend' formed the largest area of houses, fields and orchards and was a natural defensive position for the Germans, which was firmly held by 18 or 19 *Fallschirmjäger* Regiment. This large area was too big for a single battalion to take and clear and, consequently, Divisional HQ needed to coordinated an attack on the eastern portion of the village by elements of 227 Highland Brigade. While this was coordinate, there would be another pause in operations.

Meanwhile, the XVIII US Airborne Corps had dropped into their DZs.

CHAPTER FIVE

The Fly-in

By midday on 23 March the meteorologists were confirming that it looked as if the weather would enable Operation VARSITY to take place the following day and information and plans previously held at company level were briefed to the soldiers of the Division. Private Taylor of 12 Devons was one of many who recalled the final briefings in East Anglia:

> We had been dispersed to departure airfields a week or so before the battle. I think we were somewhere in Essex and the name of Mushroom Farm sticks in my memory; anyway we were living in huts there and eating RAF rations out of our mess tins. We knew that we were going into action again, but we had no idea exactly where. We were soon to find out though, because everyone was called to the briefing the day before. It was the 23 March 1945. I remember it so well because it was my 18th birthday and I was thinking, what a birthday present, I won't forget this one!
>
> The briefing was very thorough and every man jack of us knew exactly what we had to do. There was a superb model of the small

A platoon commander of one of 3 Para Brigade's two British battalions, briefs his men about DZ A.

Glider tow-ropes are prepared by ground crew at one of the departure airfields.

Last minute briefing for glider pilots, including several RAF pilots and signals personnel with side hats. (left of centre)

country town, Hamminkeln near Wesel which was to be the Battalion's battleground. Our company objective was the main crossroads in the town centre. From this model we could see quite clearly the houses and the roads, and one landmark, which I was later to recall; the Church.

Later that day the whole Battalion was called on parade: the Brigadier was to speak to us. I recall much of what he said, 'I know you have a reputation for killing the enemy, so tomorrow, get stuck in and do your job.' He then went on to specifically ask commanders not to use smoke after we landed, as it might confuse following waves of gliders who might not recognise their landing areas if there was too much of it. He wished us luck and moved off presumably to other units in the brigade.

The responsibility for lifting 6th Airborne Division was as follows:

(a) 38 and 46 Groups, RAF, would undertake all glider towing.

(b) Three Groups of 52 Wing IX USTCC would undertake all parachute drops.

The lifting of 17 US Airborne Div from the continent was allocated to [two and a half groups of] *IX USTCC.*

The total number of aircraft allocated to 6th Airborne Division was 243 parachute aircraft, mainly DC-47 Dakota aircraft, and 440 glider tug combinations of various types.

Operation Varsity D-Day 24 March 1945

As predicted the day dawned clear and fine. The post operational report recorded:

There was no early morning mist or fog, and weather at all bases was fit for take off. Visibility was good even at 0600 hours, and soon improved to 10-12 miles. There was no cloud and the flight to the target was made in perfect conditions.

While the Scottish infantry and commandos were fighting to establish a bridgehead east of the Rhine, back in the UK, 6th Airborne Division prepared to leave their transit camps on the morning of 24 March 1945, the Operation PLUNDER/VARSITY D Day. First up and getting ready, were the units of the Airlanding Brigades who in their slower tug/glider combinations would start taking off towed by an obsolescent bomber or Dakota aircraft, from 0600 hours. 12 Devons were roused by the camp tannoy at 0330 hours, and 'after an unappetising breakfast', mounted their

Hamilcars and Stirlings lined up ready to get off the ground as quickly as possible from RAF Woodbridge.

transport and dispersed to their three departure airfields; Great Dunmow, Rivenhall and Matching. Private Taylor had a restless nights sleep at Mushroom Farm Camp. This was to be his third operational deployment and knew what to expect.

> *Reveille was at 3 a.m. next morning. We were up and quickly washed and shaved and our kit packed. It was cold and bleak as my pal and I returned from breakfast at 4.15 a.m. and I recall the clanking of mess tins as the men walked to and from the cookhouse. Shortly after, we were assembled and taken to the airfield and dropped alongside our glider. In the half light of dawn we could see it and the tow rope looped in waves on the ground in front, and just ahead, our tug aircraft, a Stirling bomber. Tugs and gliders were lined up each side of the runway. This system allows for a very quick takeoff, one from the left and the next from the right until the whole group in that particular flight was airborne. They were then able to take up their flying formation with the minimum delay.*

The process of the heavily laden infantrymen climbing aboard their Mark II Horsa gliders was by all accounts 'a very much of a matter of fact nature, with the comforting proximity of companions seated shoulder to shoulder, face to face … like a crowded tube train in the rush hour'. Waiting by the aircraft, Private Taylor and the rest of his platoon of Swedebashers were ordered into the aircraft.

It was time to load up and we took our places. I was the two inch mortar man, and with my No.2 we were near the front of the aircraft with platoon HQ and the platoon commander almost opposite the front door. I could look into the cockpit and when we were flying, see the tow rope and when I leaned forward the tug too. Just before take off the tug pilot poked his head in the door and wished us good luck, cheerfully adding that he was glad he was not landing with us. The door was fastened and shortly we felt the jerk as we were towed out onto the runway, and ever faster as the tug increased power. The glider became airborne first being lighter, and we swung from side to side as the glider pilot settled down to his work holding the heavily laden glider in the correct position.

I have forgotten most of the names of my companions except for the first names of those to whom I had been close, but there was my friend Tom Gittings, Allibone (my No.2), and I recall … Stevenson who during the flight continually kept our spirits up by pretending to be airsick and making conspicuous use of the vomit bag. … I think most of us were a little apprehensive, I always was before going into action, but I had learned that as soon as we had actually started to move, all fear and dismal thoughts of getting wounded or killed disappeared as we threw ourselves into the job. It is the waiting that is hard.

However, the tension got the better of one man, as recalled by John Davis of the Ox and Bucks:

At the point of boarding our glider one of our colleague's nerves cracked and he refused to enter, whereupon RAF escorts were

The first troops making their way to the lined up Horsas.

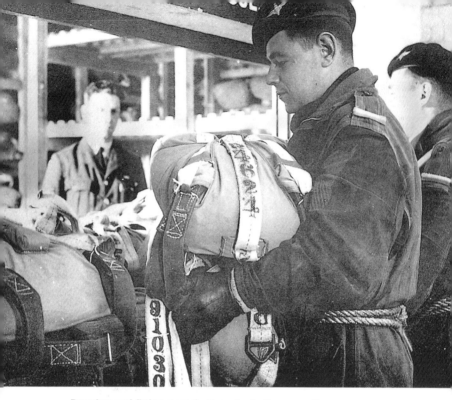

Drawing and fitting parachutes prior to the operation.

summoned – to see him being marched away was without doubt the low point of the whole operation for us …'

In common with other Brigade units, 2nd Ox and Bucks Light Infantry, taking off from RAF Birch had the usual glider towing problems. RAF glider pilot Stan Jarvis explained how he:

… began to rapidly roll down the runway. I was about fifth in order of take-off and was towed by Squadron leader Alex Blyth, from No 233 Squadron. As we gathered speed down the runway the tow-rope broke and take-off was aborted. I cleared the runway quickly by steering onto a perimeter track and the other combinations roared ahead. Alex Blyth meanwhile had managed to supply sufficient brake-power before his Dakota ran out of runway!

After the other 59 combinations had departed we were hitched up with a brand new tow-rope and then successfully took off without further incident. I carried 26 airborne troops of the Ox & Bucks Light Infantry, together with a handcart of ammunition etc. and it goes without saying that they were not best-pleased about the mishap with the tow rope.

Harry Clark was with one of the platoons of D Company 2 Ox and Bucks that had taken part in the *coup de main* against Pegasus Bridge in Normandy, also suffered a broken tow rope.

We arrived at Birch airfield at approx 0515 hours in the morning …. The Horsa gliders were lined up ready for take-off on our arrival. We roared down the runway behind a Dakota shortly after 0700 hours on a bright cold morning. We had only been airborne a few seconds when the towrope broke and we did an emergency landing back at Birch. We were quickly pulled back to the runway by a tractor, fitted with a new tow rope and were airborne again by 0620 hours.

Despite these dramas at Birch and the other RAF stations, the post operational report lists a single glider failing to get away from its base and summarises the losses *en route* to the Rhine:

> *Thirty-five gliders failed to reach the target area due to causes other than enemy action; of these sixteen were prematurely released owing to slipstream trouble, nine due to broken tow ropes, eight due to technical failure, one was late taking off and one failed to take off.*

12 Devons, being towed by Stirling tugs of an Operational Readiness and Training Squadron, who were specially mobilised for the operation, lost five gliders. Of these, only one eventually reached the landing zone east of the Rhine but, critically, the Devons had lost part of both their anti-tank and mortar platoons.

The 242 C-47 and C-53 parachute aircraft of the American 52 Wing were, meanwhile, preparing to take off from Boreham, Wetherfield and Chipping Ongar airfields. They already had the jettison supply containers fitted under their wings and their load masters waited for the arrival of the soldiers of 3 and 5 Parachute Brigades at their aircraft.

The history of 224 Parachute Field Ambulance RAMC recounted:

> *The familiar routine was followed. They put on their Mae Wests and parachute, queued for tea, then paraded for the final check and distribution of anti-seasickness pills. It was a situation that annihilated personality and distinction of rank; the individual lost in clothes and equipment, awkwardly waddling, trying to look calm and businesslike.*
>
> *At last an unseen loudspeaker crackled and cleared its throat: "Emplane as soon as possible". They heaved themselves into the aircraft, eighteen to each Dakota, and sat down uncomfortably side by side ... All along the line American dispatchers were testing the inter comms, the pilots were discussing final details with stick commander: "I'll give you a four minute red light: Okay?" The Yanks radiated a matter of fact confidence, well suited to the fleeting but vital relationship between parachutist and air crews.*

Take off was to begin at 0700 hours and in virtually every case the leading aircraft were circling for some time before the last was off the ground; '... the spluttering of engines changed to a roar, and

Airborne and in good heart on the way to the Rhine.

the whole fuselage quivered as speed increased along the runway'.

During the take-off from Wethersfield, a German V-1 flying bomb made its way into East Anglia. They '… watched a buzz-bomb chugging slowly across Wethersfield airfield beneath the circling Dakotas. It looked so lonely and so ludicrous that they could only smile at the sight, and it continued unmolested on its way like a cockroach that no one has the heart to stamp on'.

1st Canadian Parachute Battalion's historian described the flight to the Rhine aboard the thirty-five C-47 aircraft assigned to the battalion.

> *For many on board it was their first parachute drop into action, and for some, their first encounter with the enemy. For the older battle tested men in the aircraft it was a sombre time; for the untested it was a time for carefree outward calm, and a masking of inner fears and excitement with a forced smile. But for all, it was a time to check equipment and to converse with stick commanders, who had a few words with each man in his stick as the aircraft droned on towards the Rhine.*

Private Taylor continues his account of the launching of VARSITY, with a vivid description of what it was like to be aboard a glider.

91

We were flying in familiar gliders, the Horsa; it would carry just one platoon fully armed and ready for action. The British used it for troop carrying, and a larger glider, the Hamilcar, for small tanks and guns and other vehicles. It was made of plywood mostly, and flying in it would put the wind up the most experienced traveller, fondly known as the flying coffin. They would creak and groan and make the most horrifying noises as the stresses of flying tested the structure and joints, these sounds were alarming to first time flyers in the otherwise silent flight of the glider.

At times the glider pilot would decide to alter position. One normally flew above or below the slipstream of the tug aircraft which avoided the worst of the movement; any change however meant flying through this slipstream and although this normally was not too bad, frequently the glider was tossed about like a leaf in the wind. Also, just like towing a car, the glider would sometimes move up on the tug aircraft allowing the tow rope to slacken off, and when the tug took up the tow again the subsequent jerk seemed enough to pull the wings off. The sequence would be repeated for half a dozen times until normal towing was resumed and the terrified passengers could relax again. Sudden air pockets could also cause a drop of twenty feet or more without warning, and one's stomach would be left up in the air somewhat like a roller coaster at the fairground. Of course we did get used to it but the issued vomit bags were in frequent use.

The stream of Dakota parachute aircraft and the Stirling, Halifax and Dakota tug aircraft of Number 38 and 46 Groups, with the gliders flown by the Glider Pilot Regiment bearing 6th Airlanding Brigade, flew south converging on point ALTAIR, just north of Folkestone and Hythe on the south coast. Crossing the Channel, they made their landfall on the Continent between Calais and Boulogne. 6th Airborne Division flew on over the battlefield of Waterloo to Wavre, south of Brussels, where they met the stream of aircraft carrying 17th US Airborne Division, who had taken-off from airfields around Paris. The transport aircraft totalled in excess of over 1,500 parachute aircraft and 1,300 tug/glider combinations, bearing nearly 17,000 men, 600 tons of ammunition and 800 vehicles and guns. The two parallel streams of aircraft bearing XVIII US Airborne Corps, headed east across liberated Europe, taking two and a half hours to pass a given point. Lieutenant Colonel Hewson of 8 Para recalled that:

The view from the cockpit of a Horsa glider.

Dakotas fly in Victory V formations. Returning aircraft can be seen at higher altitudes.

Crossing the Channel. Air sea rescue craft patrolled the route across the Channel.

The flight was uneventful. It was a sunny clear day, and occasionally during the flight, I looked through the door and saw the most impressive stream of aircraft. Over the Continent, we passed under the [slower] glider stream, which would be released half-an-hour after the parachutists.

Ahead of the streams of aircraft carrying the two airborne Divisions, the Allied air forces were active in support. The post operational report summarised:

Escort over the battle area was provided by 83 Group RAF. One thousand two hundred and twenty seven Thunderbolts and Mustangs of VIII USAAF carried out supporting sweeps ahead of the main force. Heavy bombers of VIII USAAF had made strong attacks on airfields in north-west Germany on the previous days and on D-Day before P-Hour. As a result of these counter measures, the enemy was reduced to a state of impotence in the air and no enemy air reaction was reported by the air forces.

Bombing of the immediate VARSITY area by medium bombers had to stop thirty minutes before the drop began to allow the smoke and dust to clear. However, with the streams of aircraft somewhat ahead of schedule, the bombing contributed to the obscuration of the landing area.

Seven minutes early, the first American C-47 'Dakota' aircraft, carrying Brigadier James Hill's 3 Parachute Brigade, were flying in over the Rhine. Second Army's report confirmed that 'Enemy anti-aircraft fire was moderate when the leading aircraft arrived, but became more intense for successive waves, as the enemy began to recover from the anti-flak bombardment, and the gun positions had not yet been overrun. 'The order of landing was 8 Para, Brigade HQ, 1 Canadian Para Battalion, 9 Para, a troop of 3 Para Squadron RE and elements of 224 Para Field Ambulance. These were followed later by the Brigade's glider element with the balance of the heavy equipment.

Lieutenant Colonel Hewson of 8 Para recounted that:

In the leading aircraft, flown by the American Group Colonel, was the DZ marking stick who would be responsible for putting down the coloured smoke at the battalion RV.

Marking 6th Airborne's DZs was the job of the Pathfinders of 22 Independent Parachute Company. In Normandy and at Arnhem pathfinders had been dropped twenty minutes ahead of the main drop and set up both radio and visual beacons but in this case, as they were dropping directly on top of the enemy, they would initially mark the DZs visually. In theory, the DZs would be easy to spot being close to the easily identifiable bends in Rhine, an *autobahn* under construction and woods and marking was a regarded as merely a useful backup.

Approaching 3 Parachute Brigade's DZ A, to the north of the Diesfordterwald, Colonel Hewson recalled the final minutes of the flight:

At 0946 hours, we were given the order 'Five minutes to go'. I remember feeling very apprehensive about this, as according to the time given this would mean dropping on the wrong side the RHINE. However, at 0951 hours we crossed the RHINE with the

The drop at about 800 feet.

usual sinking feeling of impending 'baling out'. I remember looking forward from the door and seeing the fog of battle on ground, the aftermath of the terrific pounding from our massed artillery.

Red light-green light-out-parachute open-ground fairly hard-sigh of relief!

Operation VARSITY had begun.

CHAPTER SIX

3 Parachute Brigade

Flak Suppression Plan – 'CARPET'

Enemy fighter capability had been attacked in the days prior to the crossing by concentrated attacks on airfields, especially those that the new Messerschmitt 272 jet aircraft where known to operate from in the area of Rhine. In the two weeks between the arrival of 21st Army Group on the banks of the Rhine and the assault crossing, there had been a significant increase in the number of flak guns in the Emmrich, Bocholt, Wesel area, to 712 light and 114 heavy (88 mm plus) anti-aircraft guns. Plans to knock out the flak before the drop and to suppress any site that opened fire during the fly-in was a key part of the plan.

83 Group, who had tactical responsibility for the whole PLUNDER area, were to oversee the destruction of enemy flak sites. Its fighter and fighter-bombers were to attack all identified anti-aircraft guns in the airborne landing area prior to P Hour. Cab ranks of aircraft dedicated to flak suppression would be operating over the DZs and LZs throughout the landing.

Second Army's artillery, armed with up to date information, thanks to the eleventh hour capture of a German flak map from the

5.5 inch guns of 8 AGRA in action, targetting enemy flak.

local anti-aircraft HQ in Wesel, would also engage flak positions up to the check-fire just before P Hour, as follows in an extract from 1 Canadian Para's war diary:

> *P-2 hrs to P-1 hr Counter-battery and softening bombardment* [BLOTTER].
> *P-30 mins to P-15 mins Anti-flak bombardment.*
> *P-15 mins to P hr Counter-battery and softening bombardment.*

The most concentrated anti-flak fire plan would take place during the thirty minutes before P Hour and involve no less than eleven field and eleven medium regiments, plus several regiments of heavies, including three US long range 155 mm battalions. With a check-fire just before P Hour, as the aircraft approached, the numbing effect of the bombardment would be at its highest for the first part of the drop. Inevitably, the gun crews would recover and be able to take on later serials, with increasing effect, which accounts for the Airlanding Brigade's fly-in casualties.

The Parachute Drop

At 0951 hours, the leading aircraft carrying 3 Para Brigade crossed the Rhine and started to drop their paratroopers. Lieutenant Colonel Hewson, of 8 Para, having survived the drop, started to

Despite the light hearted mood, most men would have been apprehensive.

Sticks of eighteen men each descend to the drop zone.

orientate himself:

> *There seemed to be very little flak, bullets were whining across the DZ, nothing compared to the mental relief of landing safely. I landed 100 yards east of the wood. The initial briefing and air photographs left no doubt as to the RV, in addition the blue smoke was already visible, the officer in Number 1 plane had dropped a few yards from the RV.*

With the American Dakota pilots flying a very concentrated formation, it took only ten minutes for the whole of 3 Para Brigade to be on the ground, with only a few of the Brigade's sticks going astray. The aircraft were, however, flying at the highest possible speed for parachuting in order to present more difficult targets and this served to spread the dropping paratroopers across the DZ.

See map
page 109

Looking up Colonel Hewson noted that there was still '... very little flak. One or two planes were shot down. I remember as I was getting out of my parachute watching a Dakota returning with flames streaming out of the engine; probably No, 1 plane flown by the Colonel, which crashed west of the Rhine'. Meanwhile, on the ground, with the battalion rendezvous (RV) being marked by smoke:

99

There was now a considerable amount of shooting on the DZ, chiefly enemy, as at this stage of a drop it would be fatal for our own troops to open up. You can imagine the sight on the DZ, thousands of parachutes drifting slowly to the ground and on the ground. Men getting out of their harness and opening kit bags with feverish haste, talking to anyone within call about the 'jump', for at this stage in an operation to have landed safely is to be inoculated with 100% morale. Blue smoke going up from the east RV to guide in 9 Pars Engineers and Bde HQ. Yellow smoke from the Canadian RV to the west. A scene of indescribable chaos, yet rapidly men were moving off to the RVs and within thirty-five minutes 85% of the Brigade had reported in. Above it all a continuous stream of aircraft flying east, the scream of 88 mm shells, the puff's of smoke in the sky, and the long lazy curves of tracer reaching at what looked a sitting target.

Once on the ground, the battalions set about completing the initial tasks Brigadier Hill had assigned to them. 8 Para secured the DZ and was then to hold the northern part of the Dieserfordterwald, 9 Para set out to seize the south-eastern part of the wood including the Schneppenburg feature, while 1 Canadian Para advanced through the trees to occupy the central area of the Forest.

As an aside, it is worth noting that the first member of 6th Airborne Division to cross the Rhine did so by LVT and that Colonel MacEwan's RAMC, the divisional medical commander already well on his way to the DZs.

Prevented by my [Major General Eric Bols's] order from travelling by air on this operation, he was the first member of the division across the Rhine bridgehead, and first to make physical contact with the troops who had landed by air.

8 Para

Even though 8 Para's drop was well concentrated, several sticks went astray one of which was the Anti-Tank Platoon who:

… had jumped to the east of the DZ, owing to a failure in the light signals in the aircraft. Returning to the DZ, they had a short sharp engagement in a house and captured an officer and fifteen men of a German signal unit together with their 3-ton lorry. This vehicle was invaluable later when the DZ had to be cleared.

On DZ A, the enemy in the woods were quickly identified by 8 Para

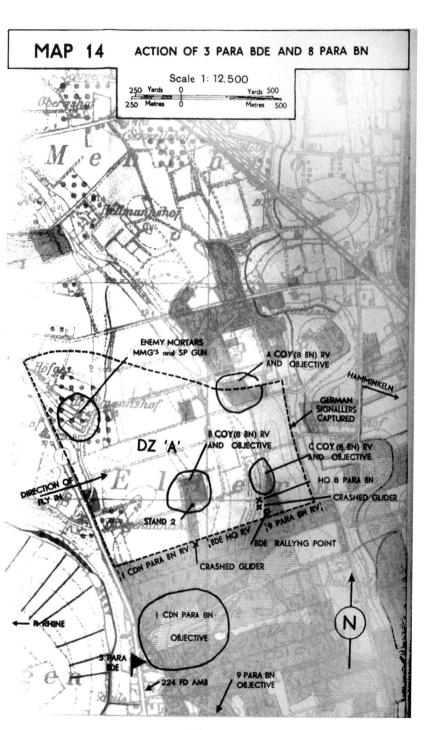

MAP 14

ACTION OF 3 PARA BDE AND 8 PARA BN

Scale 1: 12,500

ENEMY MORTARS
MMG'S and SP GUN

A COY (8 BN) RV
AND OBJECTIVE

HAMMINKELN

Höfa...

GERMAN
SIGNALLERS
CAPTURED

DZ 'A'

B COY (8 BN) RV
AND OBJECTIVE

C COY (8 BN) RV
AND OBJECTIVE

DIRECTION OF
RLY IN

HQ 8 PARA BN

CRASHED GLIDER

STAND 2

9 PARA BN RV

1 CDN PARA BN RV   BDE HQ RV   BDE RALLYING POINT

CRASHED GLIDER

N

R RHINE

1 CDN PARA BN
OBJECTIVE

3 PARA
BDE

224 FD AMB

9 PARA BN
OBJECTIVE

101

A panorama of DZA covering an arc east to north.

as *Fallschirmjäger* (The DZ was just to the north of the boundary between *7th Fallschirmjäger* Division and *84th Division*). Approximately two platoons of Germans, who were 'prepared to and actually did make a fight of it', occupied a tongue of wood (known as Axe Handle Wood) extending north from the Dieserfordterwald. This was B Company and the Machine Gun Platoon's RV and objective. As is to be expected, with the aircraft travelling faster than normal for jumping, B Company's sticks of paratroopers, though accurately dropped, were spread across the DZ. Releasing their parachute harness and recovering their fighting order and weapons, they headed towards their RV in small groups. Under fire from the Axe Handle, the first thirty or so paras to approach were gathered together by Major Kippen, who led them in an immediate and aggressive attack from the south. Both he and another officer were killed and several men were wounded

A contemporary picture of DZ A with Axe Handle Wood to the right and Wood B to the left.

in the fighting amongst the trees and trenches. Outnumbered, the remnants of the *ad hoc* platoon of paratroopers were temporarily forced back. Eventually, Axe Handle Wood was taken:

> ... *by a platoon attacking from the north-east using 36 and 77 grenades* [high explosive and white phosphorous – instant smoke] *and covered by the fire of the platoon which had earlier attempted an attack from the south. The last phase of the attack was a hand-to-hand fight down a trench, led by the platoon commander.*

At least half the *Fallschirmjäger* were killed or wounded and one officer and twenty-six Germans were taken prisoner.

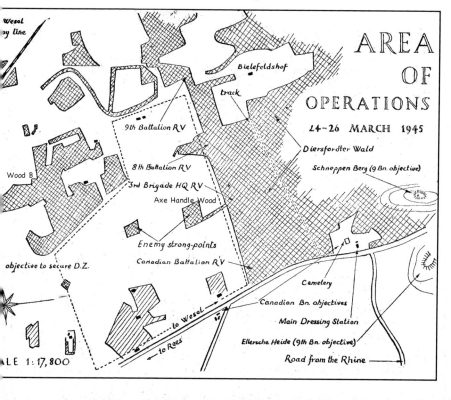

To the north-east, the tree line (Wood B) was also held and the orchards and houses to the north (Höfges) contained enemy mortars and an assault gun. Artillery and anti-aircraft detachments were scattered round the DZ and throughout the Dieserfordterwald to the south. Later an enemy officer taken prisoner told Colonel Hewson that they:

> '... expected airborne troops to be used for the RHINE crossing and it was appreciated that this DZ was one of the few places where we could safely jump. In consequence of this, it had been strongly held, but when no paratroops appeared, at 0900 hours most of them had been sent forward to counter-attack the troops crossing the Rhine. I was very glad to hear it!

This would also account for the distinct increase in tempo of German operations against the bridgehead's both 15th and 51st Divisions at about that time.

Despite the presence of a slightly depleted enemy force on and around their DZs, 3 Para Brigade assembled promptly. 8 Para's task to secure the area of the DZ was important, as the southern part of it would subsequently be used to land the Brigade's heavy equipment in vulnerable gliders. Colonel Hewson recalled that on time:

> The gliders began to arrive at 1100 hours. One of the first down, a 9th Parachute Battalion gliders, overshot the LZ but although it was badly damaged, there were no casualties ... I was standing on the edge of the wood, briefing my Intelligence Officer to keep in touch with Brigade Headquarters on the wireless, ... Suddenly, with a terrific crash, a glider came through the trees and I found myself lying under the wheel of a jeep. I managed to crawl out from the wreckage to find the glider, one of the medical Horsas of 9th Parachute Battalion, completely written off. The crew had been killed and my Intelligence Officer and two sergeants were also dead.

Colonel Hewson was very lucky to be alive. A witness said that he struggled out from under the wreckage 'madder than hell and stiff as a poker, every bone aching, yelling his famous cry "How now you whorin' bastard shite!". No one who heard him was left in any doubt that the six foot three northerner was extremely angry!'

With the volume of flak increasing noticeably, another flight of gliders came in from the south west.

At 1115 hours, the battalion's Hamilcar glider arrived, bringing in a very welcome load of a Bren carrier, spare 3-inch mortars, Vickers medium machine guns and some radio sets. Shortly afterwards, the enemy began to bring down shell and mortar fire on the drop zone. However, the battalion continued to clear it of equipment and containers, almost completing the task by 1200 hours at which time it was ordered into brigade reserve. It subsequently moved off from the DZ, leaving one platoon from C Company to finish clearing equipment from the DZ and to guard the equipment dump. En route *to its new position, the battalion encountered two 88mm guns, one of which was firing into the trees and causing casualties from shrapnel bursts. Both guns, however, were attacked and knocked out.*

Either hit on the way down or as he hung in one of the trees around the DZ, this paratrooper suffered a macabre fate.

Only two of the Brigade's seven heavy Hamilcar gliders landed in the correct area, the furthest away coming down a mile north of 8 Para's cordon. Leaving the platoon of C Company to hold DZ A for the supply drops, at 1500 hours, the remainder of the battalion went into brigade/divisional reserve in the area due east of the Schneppenberg feature. However, despite the best efforts of 8 Para and the Canadians whose objective they were, a group of *Fallschirmjäger*, with both machine guns and mortars, were still ensconced in Höfges to the north-west of the DZ.

1 Canadian Para

Lieutenant Colonel Jeff Nicklin, Commanding the Canadian Paras summarised how he expected his battalion to fight in his operation order:

(a) *SPEED and INITIATIVE on part of all ranks is the order of the day.*

(b) *RISKS will be taken.*

(c) *The ENEMY will be attacked and destroyed wherever he is* found.

With these words, along with details of the task memorised by every man, the Canadian paratroopers flew across the Rhine in their Dakotas and started to jump onto DZ A, just four minutes after 8 Para. This was far from adequate for 8 Para to have cleared the area for the following waves. Flak increased significantly as the Canadians dropped and several of their aircraft were shot down, with some paratroopers managing to jump out of burning aircraft. Private Robby Robson was one of them:

At approximately 1000 hrs we parachuted under intense fire over the Drop Zone near a town called Wesel. My plane 'The Red Dog' was hit on the port side causing the engine to burst into flame making it quite 'iffy' as we had to jump through the flames of a plane out of control, and as I was second to last in the stick, I became quite anxious about getting out in time. 'The Red Dog' sadly crashed with its valiant crew.

Struggling from aircraft that the crew fought to control, left many Canadians coming down to the east of the DZ. C Company radio operator, Private Cerniuk, was one such soldier, who jumped out of a burning aircraft. Beneath his canopy, he could see the main DZ several miles distant but fortunately the enemy's attention seemed fixed on it. He did, however, receive several bursts of machine gun fire, one of which cut the rope from which his container hung and down went the radio. He managed to pull down on the left riser of his parachute harness and, spilling wind, he steered into a patch of scrub. Landing and quickly out of his harness, he

An 88mm anti aircraft gun and crew in action.

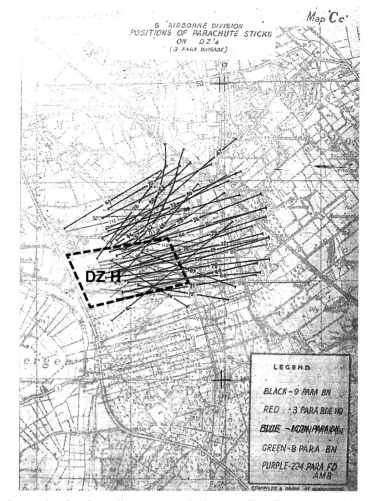

DZ H

LEGEND

BLACK – 9 PARA BN

RED – 3 PARA BDE HQ

BLUE – 1 CDN PARA BN

GREEN – 8 PARA BN

PURPLE – 224 PARA FD
AMB

A map showing the well concentrated sticks of 3 Para Brigade on DZ A.

had only his pistol and grenades, with which to defend himself. According to the battalion's historian, 'He spent the rest of the day evading the enemy but... found himself caught up in a friendly creeping artillery barrage' and surviving this linked up with the Scots who were following the barrage.

Leading the Canadian drop onto DZ A, was the main part of C Company, who also came under machine gun fire as they descended and suffered several casualties before they were on the ground. With the company commander wounded and the second-in-command killed, senior NCOs took the lead. Sergeants Saunders and Murray led members of their company in an immediate frontal attack on a *fallschirmjager* held group of houses

A damaged US Dakota aircraft crashed west of the Rhine.

on the edge of the DZ around a road/track junction (marked X on the map opposite). They organized:

> ...*a number of men that landed close to the C Company objective...into an attack formation, and charged directly into the enemy positions. The courageous attack completely routed the German gun crews, and the company objective was taken before many of the company could make their way from the Drop Zone to assist.*

The enemy fire then redoubled from buildings further north in Höfges and it seemed that the attack was going to fail. Seeing this, Company Sergeant Major (CSM) Green organised some covering fire and then went forward with an assault group to the first house, which was cleared after some unpleasant hand-to-hand fighting. Further buildings were cleared of *Fallschirmjäger* in a similar manner, until the all the buildings had been captured but they were subsequently reoccupied by the enemy once the Canadians moved off.

During the drop, some Canadians were caught up in the trees surrounding the DZ including the Commanding Officer. The CO and his second-in-command Major Eadie, had arranged to jump as

Major Eadie.

they crossed the Wesel-Rees road, aiming to land west of Axe Handle Wood. Major Eadie landed under fire from a group of five Germans in the edge of the wood and cutting himself out of his harness and rolling into a furrow in the field, returned fire with his Tommy gun, before making off to the RV. The Commanding Officer, however, was missing. Eventually it was discovered that he had landed in a tree at the edge of the wood, over a *Spandau* position and was shot as he struggled in his harness. With the CO missing, his second-in-command took over command of the battalion.

HQ Company mortarman Private Dafoe reached the Battalion RV where he found Brigadier Hill

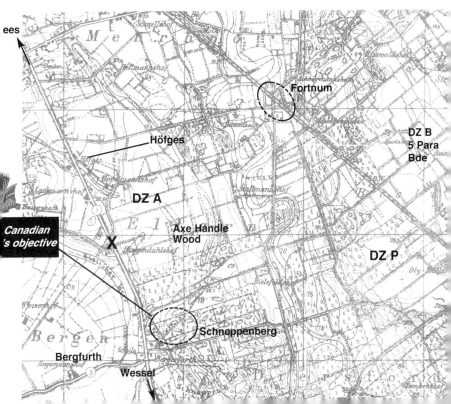

directing operations 'like a traffic policeman'. The RV came under fire from an 88mm gun and Dafoe and Private King were ordered by the Brigadier to knock it out with their mortar. The bipod legs were, however, missing having gone astray in the drop but they had trained for this eventuality.'Private King acted as observer and 'fire director', while Dafoe operated the mortar ... The first two rounds bracketed the German gun, and the third round silenced it with a direct hit.'

Despite having suffered significant losses of men and equipment during the drop, the Canadian paratroopers had assembled quickly along the northern edge of the wood bordering the DZ, and formed into viable sub-units, moved off the DZ, leaving 8 Para to deal with the enemy left in the area. They set off for their objectives a short distance to the south in the Dieserfordterwald, overlooking the Bislich-Hamminkeln road and the Wesel road, and the approach to be taken by 15th Scottish Division.

Corporal Tophan VC

Although 1st Canadian Parachute Battalion had set off from DZ A, they left elements of their medical detachment to clear casualties from the DZ, which 8 Para was still struggling to clear. The Canadian Medical Officer, appreciating the difficulties of casualty evacuation, had selected the biggest and strongest men to be trained as his medics; amongst them was Corporal George Topham, a pre-war miner from northern Canada. Assisting the Canadians was a section of medics from 224 Parachute Field Ambulance. Two of these men rushed out on to the DZ, where the majority of the Canadian casualties were to rescue a wounded man but:

> A burst of enemy fire cut them down. He [Topham] ran past the mortally wounded medical orderlies to the man still lying in the exposed area. Shots rained about him as he tended the wounded soldier; one bullet ripped across his cheek and another through his nose.
>
> Toppy refused to be evacuated. He went back out there again and again and continued evacuating the drop zone until he had cleared it. It wasn't until then that he finally agreed to sit down and listen to reason and let the doctors work on him. Even then he refused to be evacuated.

Corporal Topham VC.

Later, having been treated for his face wounds, Corporal Topham was on his way back from the Regimental Aid Post and came across a knocked out Bren-gun carrier. Corporal Einarson, of the Machine Gun Platoon, was returning from Battalion HQ with fresh belts of ammunition at that moment:

I saw a man jump up on top of the carrier and literally lift the occupants out – the driver, the co-driver, and the people behind and hand them down. I thought the person was absolutely out of his mind, being up on top of the carrier when the thing was literally exploding and burning and popping underneath him. As I moved down the road, I looked back and saw him jump-off. Then the carrier exploded. The man was George Topham.

See page 205 for citation

These acts of valour earned Corporal Topham the Victoria Cross; the first awarded to 6th Airborne Division.

Selflessness is a characteristic of the Medical Services but is a quality that was not confined to British and Canadian medics. Corporal Flynn was leading a clearance patrol in the woods when he was severely wounded in the thigh. He recalls:

I called for a stretcher-bearer and a German POW, a medic, came over to take care of me. He dressed my wound, gave me my morphine that I supplied to him, and then he got the guys to come and make a very quick litter to carry me back. We were going down the road when we were shelled by mortars. This German fellow threw his body right on top of me to protect me. He took me to 224th Field Ambulance and that was the last I saw of him; I guess he saved my life.

Dieserfordterwald

Meanwhile, Major Eadie was leading the Canadian paratroopers off to complete their tasks. The central area of the Dieserfordterwald consisted of the western edge of the woods, including the main road (now the B8) running north from the Wesel to Rees, and a number of houses. It was thought that this area was held by *Fallschirmjäger,* as the German's inter-divisional boundary was in this area. The extract from the 1 Canadian Para's

Operation order gives the company tasks in this phase of the operation. The capital letters in brackets reference the map below:

Tasks

34. C Coy

   (a) *Immediately on landing will rush, seize, clear and hold area rd junc 154478 (A) (one pl) and area corner of wood 155477 (B) (two pls). Success code word of this objective 'HANSON'*

35. A Coy

   (a) *Immediately on landing will rush, seize and clear R.V. area edge of woods map ref 157477 (B).*

   (b) *On success word 'HANSON' being recd A Coy on orders of Bn H.Q. A Party will move through woods along edge to C Coy area, corner of wood 155477 (B).*

   (c) *A Coy will pass through C Coy area (2 pls) and move SOUTH in woods along edge of rd towards area houses 156472 (C) with object to clean and hold this area (156472) (C).*

   (d) *Consolidation - A Coy will consolidate area X rds 158473 (D) - houses area 156472 (C)– rd junc 156474 (E) - track and trail X rds 158474 (F).*

36. B Coy

   (a) *Immediately on landing will rush, seize and clear R.V. Area 158477 (A).*

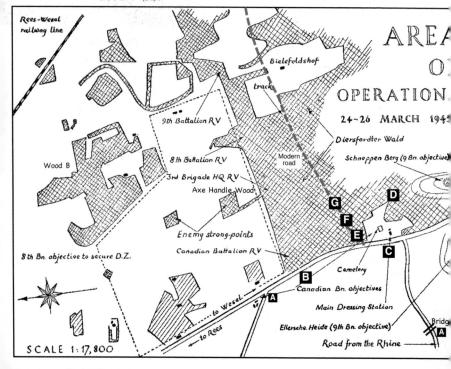

Brigadier Hill visiting his units at the dug-in on the edge of Dieserfordterwald.

(b) On success code word HANSON being recd B Coy on orders of Bn H.Q. A Party will move SOUTH-WEST along track through woods to F.U.P. area X rds 158473 (D) in anticipation of flank attack on area bldgs 156472 (C).

(c) One Pl B Coy will seize clear and hold area X rds houses 156472(C) on reaching F.U.P.

(d) On area houses 156472 (C) being cleared by either A Coy or B Coy - B Coy will consolidate area 160472 - 159470 (G) - wood and junc 157469 - rd junc 156472 (C).

In summary:

C Company was first to clear the road junction and corner of the woods in the northern sector. A Company would then pass through C Company in order to clear and hold the area of the houses where Bn H.Q. would later be established. B Company was to move south-west through the woods to provide flank protection, to seize and hold the cross roads about which the houses were grouped, and to consolidate the southern sector. All companies would then carry out extensive local patrolling for their own protection and in order to attempt to establish contact with British and American troops.

Virtually all of A Company dropped east of DZ A and they duly moved south through the woods but not before B Company, commanded by Captain McGowan, had pushed through the woods and attacked a group of farm buildings and a wooded area from which the enemy was already bringing fire to bear on the company. Under covering fire from their Bren guns, B Company assaulted and overran the enemy positions, which included a trenches and bunker system. 'The enemy were flushed out by a copious use of grenades'. CSM Kemp led an attack on the farmhouse itself under very heavy fire. In less than thirty minutes from the drop, B Company's objective was secure.

The Battalion was reporting that it had secured its objective at 1130 hours. In the process of clearing their part of the Dieserfordterwald, the Canadians had destroyed several German artillery gun positions. Major Eadie recalled that:

B Coy took large numbers of prisoners, which constituted quite a problem because they numbered almost the strength of the Bn. It was fortunate that Germans were killed by the hundreds, otherwise it would have been impossible to corral and guard them in the early hours of the operation.

9 Para

After an uneventful flight, during which, Lieutenant Colonel Napier Crookenden was awakened by the cry of the crew 'twenty minutes to go'. At about 1015 hours, with a shout in of 'Green on! Go!' in my left ear [which] sent me out into the sunlight'. He was the first man of his battalion to jump.

The ground below was already covered with parachutes of the 8th Battalion and 1st Canadian Para and I could see them running to their objectives. There was a continuous rattle of machine gun fire and the occasional thump of a mortar or grenade during my peaceful minute of descent.

As the commanding officer landed, he heard the crack of two bullets; near misses. Forty-five minutes later he had collected about 85% of his battalion's drop strength and moved off, at 1100 hours, with Major Parry's A Company leading, to capture the Schneppenberg feature in the south-western part of the Dieserfordterwald. An hour later, the northern part of the feature had been cleared by A Company with only light opposition and twenty-two prisoners were taken. The southern part of the objective was clear by 1300 hours, with an enemy SP gun being knocked out and B Company attacking and capturing a battery of towed 75mm guns positioned on the edge of the wood who were firing at 15th Scottish Division. In the process of reaching and clearing their objectives, 9 Para took some two hundred and thirty prisoners.

Major Alan Parry.

9 Para had successfully established itself in the wooded area south of the Canadians by 1330 hours. In detail, A Company remained on the Schneppenberg, B Company was digging in covering the Wesel-Emmrich road, while C Company were in the wood to the south of the road. As with the Canadians, 9 Para had to hold this large and densely wooded area with patrols. Meanwhile, as already recorded, 8 Para moved from DZ A to a position in the wood to the east of the other two battalions. They reported that they were in their new location at 1500 hours.

At 1530 hours, 9 Para dispatched a patrol to contact 2/513 US Parachute Infantry Regiment whose objective were further to the south-west down the Wesel-Emmrich road. Meanwhile, 15th Scottish Division was securely across the Rhine and was holding a bridgehead approximately two miles deep but there was a gap of a mile or more of open ground to the Dieserfordterwald and 3 Para Brigade's positions. Patrols were deployed by all three of 44 Lowland Brigade's battalions to make the initial link up. 6 King's Own Scottish Border, having least far to go, contacted 507 Parachute Infantry Regiment in the village of Dieserfordter at 1400 hours and further south, 6 Royal Scots Fusiliers joined the Americans at 1510. Yellow Celanese triangles were carried by all ranks of the assault brigades and radio contact frequencies were allocated to reduce the likelihood of 'blue on blue' or 'friendly fire' incidents. 8 Royal Scots reached 6th British Airborne Division near Bergen at 1515 hours, having secured the small Bridge A *en route*. The all important link up had been made. This enabled the airborne troops to concentrate on facing the threat of XLVII *Panzerkorps* from the east across the River Issel and for 15th Scottish Division to place their main effort further north with the aim of extending the bridgehead, keeping *II Fallschirmjäger Korps* at bay and closing up to the Issel.

A welcome sight, a jock from 15th Scottish Division.

CHAPTER SEVEN

5 Parachute Brigade

Heading for DZ B, just over fifteen minutes behind the leading elements of 3 Para Brigade, Brigadier Poett's 5 Para Brigade aboard 121 aircraft, received a warm welcome from increasing volumes of enemy flak. Consequently, the drop was not as well concentrated as that of 3 Para Brigade. At least two planes were hit on the final approach to the DZ and went down, while others flew on damaged to drop their paratroopers. Having dropped their load, the American Dakotas of 52 Wing, IX US Troop Carrier Command, turned in a loop to the north before heading back to the west. In doing so, however, they crossed the boundary into the heart of 7th *Fallschrimjager* Division's positions, where they received even heavier flak. In all, seventy, almost all the parachute aircraft, were hit and damaged, ten of the US aircraft were shot down east of the Rhine and a further seven crashed during the return flight.

See map
page 127

According to 5 Para Brigade's operation order their task was:
5 Para Brigade will:

> a) *Seize and hold ground astride rd from incl rd junc 197493 to incl rd junc 187497 and deny movement of enemy through the area.*
>
> b) *Secure x rds 167492 and deny passage of enemy res from the NORTH.*

To assist the Brigade, there would be the normal attachments of engineers and medics but in this case the Royal Artillery were also well represented, with not only parties from the Airborne Forward Observation unit but also eight 17-pounder and a further eight 6-pounder anti-tank guns. The smaller guns, modified to reduce width for loading in gliders, would land behind the parachute element aboard Horsas, while the 17-pounder, a little heralded British equivalent of the German 88-mm, would be delivered to battle aboard the mighty Hamilcar gliders.

Brigadier Poett recounted:

> *The Brigade had on call one medium regiment from the west bank of the river and one battery of 53 Airlanding Lt Regt, which was*

The drop of 5 Para Brigade.

to come down in gliders. The Brigade objective was beyond the reach of field artillery on the west bank'.

Lieutenant Colonel Geoffrey Pine-Coffin, like his divisional commander, also a Devonshire Regiment officer, commented on the airborne concept of operations:

The enemy in this area would be automatically taken on during the forming up process and it was hoped that the sight of a massed drop would so lower his morale that this would not be too difficult. We all hoped very hard that this would be so because a parachute battalion is very vulnerable indeed until it has formed up – in fact it doesn't exist at all; it is just a collection of individuals, or at best small formed armed bodies of men, moving in the general direction of the RV. To land on top of, or even within small arms range of, an enemy position had long been a parachutist's nightmare. But on this occasion we did it and got away with it too!

Brigade HQ was first to jump at around 1010, followed by 13 and 12 Para Battalions, 225 Para Field Ambulance, part of 591 Parachute Squadron RE and 7 Para, followed by the remainder of 591. In this case jumping almost last 7 Para was to remain in the area to secure the DZ (covering north and east) for the Brigade's gliders and supply drop and remain there until 12 and 13 Para had secured their objectives and Brigade position was established. Specified tasks included mounting a standing patrol at an important road and rail crossing in an opening in the big wood between the two Brigades, codenamed FORTNUM. Details of this task will be explained later in this chapter.

Brigadier Poett commented on 5 Para Brigade's landing and assembly:

> *Although all three battalions had been dropped accurately [but a little to the east], individual officers and men experienced considerable trouble in working out their exact positions. This period on the DZ was where most of our casualties occurred. Once enemy positions had been located and action taken to deal with them, the troops in them generally surrendered without putting up a serious fight …*
>
> *Just as our chaps were reaching their RVs, the glider borne element of the Brigade Group began to approach its landing zone … This caused a considerable diversion of enemy*

A light anti-aircraft gun is towed away from its Horsa.

artillery fire and provided a most welcome relief for us. ...thus only a comparatively small proportion of our anti-tank guns and vehicles carrying the machine guns, mortars and ammunition reached the battalions at their RVs.

Considering the circumstances of the landing, our casualties had not been unduly heavy. Our losses were approximately twenty per cent of those who had jumped.

Rather than using coloured smoke to rally the paratroopers to their respective RVs around DZ B, 5 Para Brigade used visual and sound, namely bugles and hunting horns. The Brigade's operation order laid down the unique calls:

Recognition Aids.

a) 7 Para Bn	*Green scrim*	*Bugle*
b) 12 Para Bn	*Blue scrim*	*Siren whistles*
HQ 5 Para Bde		
592 Para Sqn RE		
c) 13 Para Bn	*Red scrim*	*Hunting horn*
225 Para Fd Amb		
d) Glider pilots	*White handkerchief*	

The author of 6th Airborne Division's report commented: 'It is considered that the latter were quite inadequate and the use of smoke and 10-star rocket signals are essential'.

About an hour after the drop, the three battalions were sufficiently complete in their RVs for the Brigade to be able to report that they were ready to start on the second phase of the plan: the securing and consolidating of the Brigade's objectives.

5 Para Brigade was to protect the northern front of the Airborne Corps area by securing Area B1 and, once in position, 12 and 13 Para were to both cover likely enemy counter-attack routes into the divisional area. When its task on the DZ was complete, 7 Para was to pull back into Brigade reserve.

See map
page 125

Meanwhile, the Brigade's signallers were establishing communication. They had jumped with the new, more powerful No. 52 sets in their kit bags. The communications lessons of Arnhem had been learned and there was a sixty percent reserve of this more powerful rear link set. Where necessary, the risk was

A panoramic view east across DZ B. The tree line now hides the autobhan.

taken with opening radio frequencies having been 'netted by pre-checked crystal wave meters, and the dials locked and sealed before loading'. The risk of compromise of communications security was outweighed by the need for the passage of information from the outset. Not only had the inadequacies of radios on previous airborne operations been addressed but measures were taken to ensure liaison had taken place between Royal Signals officers within Second Army and 6th Airborne Division. In addition, the necessity of the airborne troops having all the Communication Electronic Instructions (CEIs) from relieving and flanking formations had been recognised. The CEIs were at divisional level protected by special ciphers and, at brigade level, they were concealed from enemy eyes in the hollow tubes of radio antennas.

Once on the ground, even though the Brigade Signals Officer, Lieutenant Crawford, was killed on the DZ, radio sets were quickly netted in and communications established. Crucially, the parachute elements of the Forward Observation Unit (FOU) RA were soon speaking to FOU liaison officers at artillery HQs and at medium gun positions west of the Rhine.

Meanwhile, Brigadier Poett had taken the precaution of procuring American types of walkie-talkie radios for himself and his battalion's commanding officers, which enabled effective communication within the command group. He believes that use of the walkie-talkies cut up to thirty minutes off the passage of information from an event happening to it being reported over the formal Brigade radio net. The value of timely information

Brigadier Poett.

Lieutenant Colonel Geoffrey Pine Coffin.

again outweighed the risk of enemy eaves-dropping. Colonel Pine Coffin commented that they: *'dispensed with all the mumbo-jumbo of RT procedure. There were no link signs … and no station acted as control, it was in fact, a signaller's horror but it worked and worked well too'.*

7 Para

Amongst those to jump with 5 Parachute Brigade was 7 (Yorkshire Light Infantry) Parachute Battalion, its commanding officer, Lieutenant Colonel Geoffrey Pine Coffin, described his battalion's task:

My battalion was ordered to establish itself at this end of the DZ and to take on all opposition which might interfere with the other two battalions, which were to capture the brigade objective. In short, 7 Para Bn came down looking for a fight, which is not a bad role for any battalion.

Unusually, even for a plan that envisaged vertically enveloping the enemy, 7 Para was to jump on to its objective! It is usual for a parachute battalion to form up at a battalion RV and then to set out on its task from there, but 'in this operation speed was even more important than usual and particularly so in the case of this battalion'. Therefore, in order to save time, Colonel Pine Coffin, ordered the companies to drop and form-up by themselves in the position they were to hold i.e. their objectives; 'this meant that the positions, were manned about thirty minutes sooner than they would otherwise have been'.

The approach to DZ and the drop of battalion was similar to the rest of the brigade, other than the fact that A Company overshot and assembled where they were before moving in an organised body to the their correct RV/objective. As recounted by the Commanding Officer, however, one A Company paratrooper had a lucky escape when he was at his most vulnerable.

At the risk of creating a wrong impression about the opposition, I would like to tell you the story of one of my NCOs who was dropped in the country beyond the DZ. As this man was coming down he could see someone on the ground just about where be expected to land, and, as he got lower, he could see that it was a German parachutist and that he had a Schmeisser in his hands.

There was really nothing he could do about it and so ho just cursed his luck and landed in a heap, as one does, at the German's feet. He told me afterwards that he shut his eyes and waited for the burst from the Schmeisser *but it was so long in coming that he opened them again to see what the hitch was. He found that the German was busy collapsing his chute for him and when he had done this he helped him out of his harness and unpacked his Bren gun from the kit bag – he then surrendered to him. When he had got over the shock of all this, the NCO noticed that about twenty more Germans had arrived and they all surrendered to him too. At the same time and within a mile of all this, other parties of Germans were putting up desperate fights.*

The first man to arrive at the small wood that was to be the RV of

A vital piece of equipment to an otherwise lightly armed parachute battalion: the Vickers machine gun.

HQ Company was the company commander. He had worked out his jumping order with very great care so as to land as close to the RV as possible; 'he got it a bit too accurate because he came down actually on it and got caught up in one of the trees'. Unlike Colonel Nicklin, he freed himself and was busy searching the wood for enemy when the first of his paratroopers arrived. 'They said that he was doing this quite thoroughly, except that he had forgotten to put a magazine on his Sten!' Fortunately, there were no Germans in this particular area, presumably they too had been called forward to the river line but they had clearly been there a short time before and had as one paratrooper commented '...dug some good slit trenches which saved us a lot of bother'.

Coming in slightly later than they should have, A Company had the worst time securing and holding their objective. When they arrived, they found that their area was 'a very nasty spot'. According to Colonel Pine Coffin, a pair of 88 mm guns firing in the ground role, located in a little wood about 700 yards to the east, just to the west of the autobahn, and commanded by a *Luftwaffe* officer:

> ... that one could not help but admire. When the drop took place it appears that the gun crews panicked and ran away but this officer managed to turn enough of them back to man one of the guns. He was of course, in a hopeless position but he kept that gun firing and did an immense amount of damage before he was rounded up. Although A Coy suffered badly, 12 Para Battalion and Brigade HQ ... got it worse.

A Company's casualties were heavy, as were those of the mortars and machine gun sections that dropped with them.

Overall, the drop achieved the desired surprise and the Germans were paralysed by the envelopment and were slow to react. According to the CO, 'The battalion was in this position (area of DZ B) for five hours and during that time there was no really serious attack put in on us'. There were, however, smaller attacks on B Company by enemy of about platoon strength and, at one point, C Company engaged and broke up a company of *Fallschrimjager* that was working its way round to attack them in a flank. 7 Para, fighting from shallow shell scrapes, remained the focus of the *Fallschirmjäger's* probing attacks but they successfully provided time for the remainder of the Brigade to dig in properly.

Battalion HQ also received the attention from the enemy and

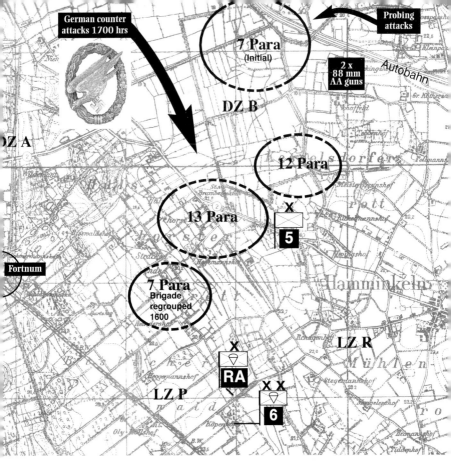

5 Para Brigade – 24 March 1945.

suffered quite a few casualties, including Colonel Pine Coffin, who lost the tip of his nose to a shell splinter, which was a painful but not debilitating wound. Colonel Pine Coffin reminds us that:

> 7 Para Battalion was to operate in this position…to assist the other battalions to seize the Brigade objective; it was not intended that it should stay here indefinitely. I am glad to be able to say that the only Germans encountered on the main [Brigade] objective were those that were already there when the landings took place; any that went there from this direction went as prisoners.

13 Para

The Battalion's war diary records that:

> 0630 hours.   Unit took of in 33 DAKOTAS and 2 Horsas from

The aircraft carrying the 585 strong 13 Para, found the area east of the Rhine shrouded with a combination of smoke, spring mist and dust from the bombardment that obscured many of the landmarks. Consequently, they were dropped, at 1010 hours, slightly east of DZ B and were promptly engaged by enemy artillery. In the confusion of orientating themselves, it took 13 Para some time to locate the enemy but when organised fire was brought down on the Germans and they saw the paratroopers forming up to assault, they promptly surrendered. A Company's commander, Major Watson, recalled:

> *Once we were on the ground, we were immediately faced with the enemy. One of my platoons to my left captured a machine gun position and we started taking prisoners – the Germans were giving themselves up all over the place. Although there was a lot of firing going on, even 88mm guns being used in the ground target role, one seemed to be oblivious to what was happening because once one had landed, one was in action straight away. There was the objective and that is what we went for – wearing our red berets and shouting our heads off.*

Because of this immediate ground action, the Brigade was slightly delayed in assembling at their RV but the use of hunting horns by the companies, each with a distinctive call, not withstanding previous comments, helped considerably.

Moving off to their objective a mile to the south-east of their RV, around a junction on the road to Hamminkeln, the battalion witnessed some harrowing sights:

> *… the saddest thing I saw was when we were moving towards our battalion objective. There were glider pilots still sitting in their cockpits, having been roasted alive after their gliders had caught fire. One pilot and co-pilot were still sitting there with their hands on their control columns. A lot of people were lost like that. Although we lost a quite lot of casualties in the air, it was nowhere near those of the glider borne troops.*

The enemy, such as they were, concentrated around the farms but the Battalion was able to dig-in as ordered on its objective. The battalion war diary recorded:

> *1500. A Company outpost counter-attacked; strength one company. 35 enemy killed and attack beaten off.*

An RAMC officer supervises PoWs recovering a wounded German soldier for treatment in the British medical chain.

By last light the situation was quiet apart from spasmodic shelling. Enemy made no attempt to counter-attack during the night.

The Royal Engineer troop of 519 Para Squadron RE, attached to the Brigade had as its principal task the opening of routes though the area for the tracked and wheeled traffic of 15th Scottish Division. This work included the clearance of enemy mines, obstacles and the filling of craters. As a corollary to this:

Very strict orders were issued in respect of mining. No anti-personnel mines were allowed, and other minefields were confined to denying the enemy egress from roads that were already planned to be blocked by necklaces of [surface laid] 75 grenades to be placed only when the approach of enemy vehicles seemed imminent.

12 Para

The thirty-three Dakotas of Ninth US Troop Carrier Command, bearing 12 Para, flew across the Rhine in very tight Victory V formations and made a successful drop. However, with so much ground obscuration, the Battalion's RVs were established at the wrong point – a very similar looking wood. Major Frank Bucher, the battalion second-in-command, led 12 Para back across the DZ to the correct location.

As the battalion crossed DZ B in single file, they came under heavy small arms fire and were shelled by the two 88mm guns to the north of the DZ. They were the same guns that was later to give A Company 7 Para considerable difficulty. Even though men were wounded by HE fire, the paratroopers pressed on leaving stretcher-bearers and medics of 225 Parachute Field Ambulance to collect the wounded.

Arriving at the correct RV, they found it was also under fire, this time from artillery at very close range. Under this fire, the companies quickly dispersed to their objectives about a thousand yards to the south. The 6th Airborne Division report commented on this and other similar incidents: 'Easily discernable landmarks such as copses should NOT be used as rendezvous, as the enemy generally knows the range and shells them'.

Major Ritchie led A Company to its objective, clearing enemy from a farm *en route*, while a platoon attacked another 88mm position and captured the guns along with their crews without loss. Having rounded up some prisoners, A Company settled down in its objective to dig-in with little serious interference.

Major Steve Stephen's C Company was, meanwhile, advancing on its objective. The leading platoon assaulted and cleared

A Luftwaffe Senior NCO anti-aircraft gunner (holder of the Iron Cross First Class) is questioned by a British paratrooper.

buildings at the edge of the objective whilst the rest of the company followed. Taking over the lead, they secured much of the remainder of the Battalion's area.

At the same time, B Company was having difficulty reaching its objective. A large platoon of enemy were positioned in several farm buildings and had to be cleared before the objective could be taken. The company under Major 'Rip' Croker, now sent forward two platoons to take individual buildings, which was achieved after a stiff fight during which, Lieutenant Cattell was wounded for a second time. 4 Platoon, who had been held back in reserve, seized the company's objective. The remainder of the company, under the second in command, then joined them. The Company's casualties were particularly significant amongst its officers and SNCOs.

In its planned position the Battalion dug-in, officers were doing the round of their command, confirming positions chosen from maps and air photographs were suitable and tying up arcs of fire. Lieutenant Colonel Darling later wrote:

> The anti-tank layout [which] had been planned through careful stereoscopic examination of air photographs and a trace had been prepared showing the tasks and approximate positions of each machine gun platoon. The battalion locations had been planned so as to include the areas from which the anti-tank defence could be best arranged,

Colonel Darling continued:

> Towards the evening, an eerie silence fell over the DZ which had been such a noisy battleground. Enemy resistance had been completely flattened and thus I was able to ride a horse, found on one of the farms nearby, around the battalion area. Special mention must be made of the sterling work of our medical staff: Captain Wilson, who was our Medical Officer, Corporal Houghton and the stretcher-bearers, and our most respected Padre, the Reverend Joe Jenkins, all of whom tended our casualties under fire. These amounted to twenty-one killed, forty-five wounded and twenty-five missing. Many of the latter rejoined the battalion later.

The DZ and Brigade Screen

While the remainder of the Brigade were digging-in, 7 Para, as per orders, remained on the DZ, not only to provide a screen but also to receive and recover as many of the jettison containers dropped by the Dakotas. There was, however, one other task for A Company 7 Para that had been left to last. This was the securing and holding of an important road and rail junction in an opening in the big wood, code-named FORTNUM, between the two parachute brigades. This seemingly simple task was allocated to a platoon and speed was essential. However, the distance from DZ B was a mile, across ground that was likely to be held by the enemy. Lieutenant Colonel Pine Coffin rejected a bald-headed double march across country in favour of a more circumspect approach.

See map page 125

A sniper from one of the Brigade's Parachute Battalions.

I decided therefore to send off a small party with a wireless set and under an officer to spy out the land and then to send off the platoon when I knew which was the best way for it to go. The officer who was to take this party, however, was killed on the DZ and ...I had no option but to send off the platoon without any preliminary reconnaissance. It was commanded by a Lieutenant Patterson, who was one of two Canadian [CANLOAN] officers that came to me in Normandy as non-jumping reinforcements ... He reached the position after many adventures, he hung on there for 22 hours before he was relieved.

From about 1200 hours when the platoon was established at FORTNUM, the Germans attacked Lieutenant Patterson at frequently intervals, from virtually every direction, throughout the hours he was isolated from the battalion. He dealt with these 'most successfully using his own rather unorthodox methods of defence'. He sized up attacks as they developed and if it were only a weak one, he would stay where he was and beat it off. However:

> *... if it seemed stronger than he could hold off, he would use the "Patterson Method", which was as follows. He would leave the position entirely and move his platoon round to one of the flanks; then, when the enemy had struck their blow at nothing and were wondering what to do next, he would rush them from the flank. In this way, he killed a great number of Germans and captured many more.*

This was an exemplary independent platoon action and the bag of prisoners added to the substantial number 7 Para dispatched to Brigade HQ.

Once the main Brigade defensive position was established by 12 and 13 Para, and DZ B cleared of men (wounded or otherwise), equipment and stores, 7 Para was ordered to pass through the Brigade into reserve. At 1545 hours, Lieutenant Colonel Pine Coffin started moving his battalion with a view to taking up positions south of the road running north-west from Hammenkeln. This was, however, easier said than done:

See map page 125

> *The withdrawal was not particularly easy because both B and C Companies were in contact at the time. A withdrawal is not an easy manoeuvre and it seemed a most unlikely thing for a parachute battalion ever to be called upon to do. Not because we thought that we could never get the worst of a battle but because there is normally, nowhere for it to withdraw too. It has no rear. We had never practised it and anyway knew little of the method; however we managed it all right and without loss.*

The platoons and companies leapfrogged backwards covering one another as they moved keeping the enemy's heads down until they came into line with 12 Para and broke clean from the enemy and withdrew through 13 Para.

5 Para Brigade's drop had been successful and by mid afternoon, they were dug-in, complete with support weapons and artillery defensive fire tasks, ready to take on any serious German counter-attack on the divisional area from the north.

CHAPTER EIGHT

6 Airlanding Brigade

Following behind the two parachute brigades was Brigadier Bellamy's 6 Airlanding Brigade, plus those of the units attached for the operation, aboard 196 Horsa gliders. The task given to the Brigade by General Bols, was to seize the key crossings of the River Issel, for both offensive and defensive purposes, and to take important road junctions and villages. Ultimately, the Airlanding Brigade was to hold approaches into the Divisional Area from the east against armoured counter-attacks that according to intelligence assessments could be expected as early as two hours after landing.

Touching down on four separate Landing Zones (LZs), 6 Airlanding Brigade's tasks, according to the 1947 British Army of the Rhine battlefield tour, were, in order of priority:

> *(i) Seize and hold certain bridges over the River ISSEL (1st Battalion The Royal Ulster Rifles (1 RUR)). LZ 'X', 2nd Battalion The Oxfordshire and Buckinghamshire Light Infantry ((2 OX & BUCKS) LZ 'Y' and 'Z')*
>
> *(ii) Clear the area C2 required for Div HQ (C Coy, 12th Battalion The Devonshire Regiment (12 DEVON))*

The cockpit of the Horsa glider. The No 1 pilot sat in the right seat.

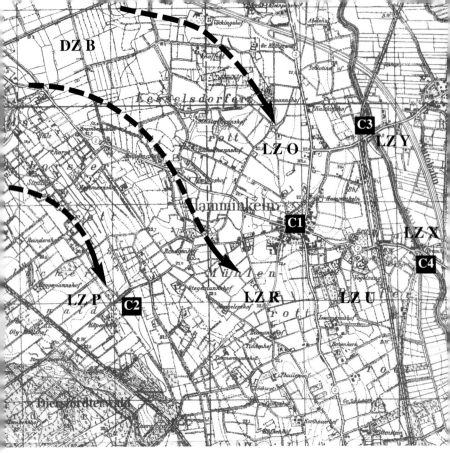

The glider fly-in routes and the objective areas.

    (iii) *Seize and hold road junction C3 (2 OX & BUCKS) and road and railway Crossing C4 (1 RUR)*

    (iv) *Seize and hold the village of HAMMINKELN (C1) (12 DEVON, which was afterwards to come into brigade reserve)*

The CRE [Commander Royal Engineers] was to coordinate the laying of anti-tank minefields as soon as possible after landing, including one designed to block the approaches to the DIERSFORDTERWALD from the North and East. This was to follow approximately the line of the 3 Para Bde/5 Para Bde and 3 Para Bde/6 Airlanding Bde boundaries. No anti-personnel mines were to be laid.

Bridges over the River ISSEL were to be prepared for demolition, but were not to be blown unless their capture by the enemy appeared certain. The decision whether or not the bridges were to be blown rested with Commander 6 Airlanding Bde.

Headquarters 6th Airlanding Brigade and C Company of 12 Devons would land on LZ P south-west of Hamminkeln (Objective C2 listed above). 12 Devons had the distinctive West Country nickname 'The Sweedbashers'.

The Landing

Gefreiter Herman Hagenberg was a member of *Flackregiment 21*, crewing a single barrel 20mm light anti-aircraft gun. He was in a newly dug position between Hamminkeln Station and the river Issel, on the southern edge of LZ O2. They had their previous location to the west of the village as a dummy position. This and others that had been abandoned duly received the full attention of the CARPET flack suppression bombardment. Hagenberg recalled:

On the morning of 24 March the sky was darkened by the countless numbers of airplanes appearing at a height of 200 metres, which were attacked by our twelve 20mm guns.

Australian Ron Hyde, piloting a Dakota 'Queen-Uncle', recalled that the visibility which had earlier been a clear twenty miles, started to fall away as they approached the river. A mix of smoke

A Luffwaffe 20mm anti-aircraft gun in its pit.

Above: A Horsa glider in flight; the principal airlanding aircraft.

Left: A C-47 Skytrain (British DC-3 Dakota) the main type used by Allied paratroopers in 1944-45.

and artificial fog hung over the Rhine, and also over Wesel there was smoke and dust from the bombing and fighting in the town. 'Grey puffs of flak were bursting just above the smoke pall, tracer and light flak were coming from underneath'. He recorded his conversation with the glider pilots as they approached release.

> 'Hello, glider. Tug calling. We're nearly at your release point. Have you picked up your pin-points?'
>
> The glider captain was straining his eyes to see through the smoke haze. Somewhere down there was his bridge, his field and his hedge.
>
> 'Glider to tug. I can just make it out.'
> 'It's pretty hazy down below. Make absolutely sure.'
> 'I will.'
> A pause – then I spoke:
> 'Tug calling. You're at release point now.'
> There was silence for fifteen seconds.

'O.K., tug. I'm right now. Cheerio.'

'Cheerio and best of luck.'

The tow-rope wrinkled like a piece of elastic and U-Q surged forward, turning sharply to get out of the press of aircraft and gliders at each side and behind. There was a crowded few minutes of near-collisions. Glider after glider disappeared into the smoke haze. Gun flashes starred the murk. I saw two Daks go down in flames. The heavy guns were out below, but there was plenty of light stuff coming in from the sides. Soon, however, we were out of it and on the return course, settled into a steady stream of returning aircraft, passing an equally steady stream of gliders and tugs carrying in more men, more guns, more equipment. And so 'U.Q' returned from her third airborne landing.

6th Airlanding Brigade's gliders were cast off from their tugs between 4,000 and 2,500 feet, starting at approx 1017 hours, and swept down, loosing a thousand feet per mile travelled. The first gliders coming in to land, at 1021 hours, were the *coup de main* force made up of soldiers from the Ox and Bucks Light Infantry, aboard eight Horsa gliders. They were followed a minute later, at 1022 hours, by seven gliders bearing the *coup de main* party of 1 RUR. The tasks of the first two flights of gliders were to capture the two road bridges and one railroad bridge over the River Issel. Next in at 1023 hours were fifty-eight Horsas carrying the remainder of the Ox and Bucks LI Group and the RUR.

At 1028 hours, the following wave of 59 Horsas started to land 12 Devons. In several groups, HQ 6 Airlanding Brigade and divisional troops landed from 1034 hours, the first in 88 Horsas and six Hamilcars. The fly-in continued with 116 Horsas and 28 Hamilcars landing around 1035 hours, and 55 Horsas and 15 Hamilcars landing at 1057 hours. Each wave presented new targets to the German anti-aircraft guns.

Private Taylor of 12 Devons described what it was like to be aboard a glider in the final approach to the LZ.

Feet up, link arms, we took up landing positions which was followed just a few seconds later by the shock of deceleration as the pilot dropped the tow. Then at first there seemed to be a silence as we lost the sound of the tug's engines; the noise of the wind roaring past decreased to a whisper as the speed dropped back, and the glider felt as if we had suddenly stopped moving. For a while, probably just fifteen seconds or so, we flew normally, and then

DZ U, with Hamminkeln windmill in the background.

*there was the loud crack of a bullet as it came through the fuselage.
We looked at one another with surprise and the sudden realisation
that this was it. Several more bullets came through the glider then
all hell seemed to be let loose.*

*Our pilot almost turned our glider into a fighter. We banked
very steeply to the right and dived at a sickening angle
corkscrewing first one way and then the other as he picked out his
landing spot. We could now hear the automatic fire and
explosions, as the enemy did their best to destroy the aircraft as we
came in to land. As we straightened out from the final spiral we
heard the shout 'stand by' and we braced ourselves for the landing.
There was a loud hard thud as we hit the field, the floor collapsed
and came up and we scraped along the ground to a bumpy stop.*

Private Taylor's glider had been luckier than many.

With the German anti-aircraft gunners having recovered from
much of the effect of the bombardment, as per orders, they
switched their fire away from the departing Dakotas of the
parachute brigades, to the four hundred incoming gliders on their

138

three to four minute flight to the fields around Hamminkeln. German operational analysts had examined the wrecked gliders around Arnhem and had been convinced by the number of bullet holes, blood in the aircraft and graves around the LZs that airlanding troops were at their most vulnerable when still aboard their gliders. Fire control orders were issued accordingly and, consequently, the Airlanding Brigade suffered cruelly from flak and other ground fire. *Gefreiter* Herman Hagenberg commented 'Our 20mm explosive shells had a terrible effect on the troops in the gliders particularly once they stopped'.

One British officer later commented that, having been assured that the flak would be fully suppressed by the CARPET bombardment and fighter bomber attacks, 'the enemy ack-ack was much greater than we had been led to expect'. Some German prisoners, however, taken during VARSITY claimed they knew the gliders were coming and that in fact they were late. After Arnhem, the planners wanted to be sure the air landing component 'went like clockwork' – in order to test the navigation beacons deployed along the route they carried out a rehearsal.

On 17 March, six Stirling/Horsa, six Halifax/Horsa and a single Hamilcar glider/tug combinations had taken-off from Great Dunmow, Earls Colne and Woodbridge respectively. They flew the exact route that was to be taken a week later, with a high-level fighter escort. Crossing into Germany but sheering off just before the Rhine, they were unmolested by enemy fighters or flak. This was a risky rehearsal, which could have compromised the operation. The Germans had expected an airborne assault about an hour after dawn.

Aboard one of the gliders allocated to carry 1 RUR, a member of a 6-pounder anti tank gun was hit by the anti-aircraft fire and recalled:

Suddenly a terrific amount of flak started to burst around us, and

A Horsa comes in to land at ninety miles an hour.

some aircraft were hit. Les and I sat in the tail section of our glider and strapped ourselves in. From where we were, we couldn't see what was going on outside. Shortly afterwards we cast off from the tug and, as we did so, there was a big explosion under us which blew a hole in the glider. Les said that he had been hit and he had a very nasty wound. My backside felt wet, and I found I was sitting in a pool of my own blood.

We immediately went into an almost vertical dive, which was the manual landing approach for a glider. However, not knowing what was happening up front, I thought that was us, going straight in. I remember saying to Les not to worry, because there was nothing we could do, and that we'd had it. I wasn't scared. Petrified, yes! But not scared. I was very relieved when I heard the noise of compressed air, which operated the air brakes, and realised that somebody was still driving us. We made a perfect landing in the middle of a huge open area, until our wheels went into a deep trench and stopped us dead. After we were down, I noticed the back of my hand was bleeding where I had dug my fingernails in.

We landed at twenty past ten, and there was still a large part of the Brigade to come in. One glider went straight into an orchard on our left, and within a short time we could see German civilians removing the bodies and laying them all together on the ground. Another glider, completely engulfed in flames, flew past with the occupants screaming, and noises, as though they were banging against the sides trying to get out. Oddly enough, it looked as though it was heading for a perfect landing.

RAF glider Pilot Stan Jarvis, who was towards the rear of the stream of aircraft, despite taking a short cut to catch up after a broken tour-rope, wrote:

When we reached the Rhine the strength of the flak became apparent. A few of the earlier tug aircraft flew past us on their way home, some of them were on fire and others were bullet ridden – not a welcoming sight to us who were going in to stay.

Enemy fire was only one of the problems facing the glider pilots. Ground obscuration was another problem, as Private Harry Clark of the Ox & Bucks` recounted:

As we crossed over the Rhine at an altitude of some 5000 feet, the river appeared as a narrow twisting silvery ribbon. The Horsa cast off from its tug aircraft about two miles over the enemy side of the river. We could see a dense wall of smoke drifting across the battlefield from the direction of Wesel and one of the pilots shouted out that the LZ was obscured by the haze and smoke. Anti-aircraft fire began to intensify as we rapidly lost altitude. We plunged into the smoke.

Stan Jarvis wrote that having been released:

At that point we could not see the ground at all, as we were technically in a cloud – but it was smoke – and we were trying to avoid other aircraft flying in our direction. My co-pilot Peter Geddes was meanwhile desperately trying to identify anything through the smoke…The first landmark which we saw was an autobahn east of Hamminkeln and at that moment there was a tremendous explosion on the starboard side and about four feet of the wing tip was blown off…

The VARSITY Post Operational Report commented that, aiming for precision landings:

The glider pilots were given an air photograph of their landing zone but in cases this photograph covered only the immediate area in which they were to land. This resulted in some pilots who had gone off course being unable to pick up their bearings. A second photograph covering a larger area would have helped.

Private Harry Clark continued his passenger's account of his glider's approach to LZ O:

The wreck of a crashed Horsa glider.

Issel Road Brigades (Objective C3)

Ringenberg

Wood Stacks

Hamminkeln Station

Autobhan

LZ U2 (see map on page 145). Ox and Bucks LI.

Most of the men in the Horsa sat silently in their seats, waiting for the certain impact of the crash landing that would shortly occur. Our glider hit the ground at approx 90mph losing the wheels on impact. Pieces of wings were torn off as we went through a series of ditches and hedges. We came to a halt and swiftly removed ourselves from the battered wreckage. I shook hands with the two pilots, who apologised for the bad landing. I remarked in my opinion 'it was a very good landing', apart from a few cuts and bruises we were all alive. Gliders were crash landing all around us. Two were destroyed within yards of our forming up position with a total loss of life. Several more were in flames with no signs of life or movement.

Meanwhile, in the mist and smoke, Sergeant Major Lawrance 'Buck' Turnbull, one of only six Glider Pilots to take part in, and survive, all four major British glider operations in World War 2, nearly came to grief in an accident over the LZ. Turnbull's epic started when a Dakota crossed his Horsa's path and dragged its tow cable over the upper surface of his aircraft, ripping his starboard aileron off! The rope then momentarily wrapped itself around the cockpit, smashed the Perspex and ripped off the air bottles that that operated the flaps and brakes. As its final act of vandalism, the towrope tore away half of the control column. By this time, the Horsa, which was fully loaded with troops, was now almost inverted. It took all Turnbull's skill and strength to regain control of the aircraft, with only the stump of the column remaining. He landed his platoon of infantry on the correct LZ and promptly went into action with his passengers! Sergeant Major Turnbull was awarded the only Conspicuous Gallantry Medal (CGM) of the Second World War.

Corporal Cooper of 195 Field Ambulance was luckier but still likened his glider's landing to 'a controlled accident' – that led many paratroopers to believe that they were better off jumping without a reserve parachute and risking the perennial DZ problems of breaks and sprains.

> *The gliders were cast off at 3000 feet and came down to ground level in three swoops. Despite the warnings received at the briefing, the under carriage of our glider did catch the power lines and we nose-dived into a ploughed field. The 'skid' a landing device in addition to the tricycle wheels was forced through the floor of our glider, later leading to difficulties in getting the jeep out.*

In one extreme case, the Quartermaster of 2 Ox and Bucks LI, Captain Aldworth, with no flying instruction, landed his glider safely with both the pilots dead or wounded at the controls. Other gliders suffered similar catastrophic failures and crashed with a total loss of life. Fifty Army and fifty-one co-opted RAF pilots were killed during the landing or on the LZs.

Casualties from flak and landing accidents were far heavy than anticipated. For example, the Ox and Bucks LI suffered badly and 'from a force of just over 600 men, we suffered some 105 killed and approx 240 wounded in the terrible landing'. This left a depleted force to carry out the battalion's task. It is also worth noting that of the 440 gliders only twenty-four were recovered in a vaguely airworthy condition with the rest being salvaged for spare parts.

Private Reg Reid of A Platoon, 133 Company RASC, was, on the west bank, waiting in a hide to cross the Rhine and witnessed the arrival of a glider that landed the wrong side of the Rhine:

> *On 24 March 1945, out trucks were waiting on the west side of the river and we saw hundreds of Dakotas going overhead which*

143

cut loose gliders carrying paras. One or two landed near us on the wrong side of the river and, it must be said, our paras `scared the blue lights' out of us. As the gliders landed, the front of these big aircraft opened and bren gunners raked the hedges we were sheltering in before realising they were firing at their own side! Jeeps and the paras then poured out and were so hyped up for battle that they headed for the riverbank, as if to swim across! The lads manhandled them away from the wide, fast flowing river. They'd have to wait, like us!

In summary, the paragraph on flak suppression in 6th Airborne Division's report reads:

It was, as a result of MARKET, confidently expected that the flak would, to a very great extent, be neutralised by the fighters and fighter bombers and by the 'Apple Pie' [CARPET] fired by 12 Corps artillery. In fact the degree of neutralisation achieved was not high and many 20mm, 40mm and 88mm guns remained in action all through the landings, taking their toll of gliders both in the air and on the ground.

Enemy flak in the area was considerable and was put there mainly in the anti-airborne role. This was stated by the commander 84 German Infantry Division, who was by no means impressed with the efforts made to neutralise it. Two factors probably contributed:

1. The smoke, haze must have handicapped the fighters.

2. The arrival of the first wave of parachute aircraft, nine minutes early which cut short the 'Apple Pie' before it had been completed.

The Coup de Main Attacks

The leading fifteen Horsa gliders were heading for three LZs adjacent to the bridges across the River Issel. The bridge carrying the Hamminkeln road east was to be captured by 1 RUR (Objective X) and a road/rail pair (Objectives Y and Z) a little further north, near Ringenburg were to be seized by 2 Ox & Bucks LI.

The Ox & Bucks's bridges were two hundred yards apart, the southerly was a road bridge allocated to Major Rahr's B Company (LZ O1), with a railway bridge just to the north, which was to be taken by C Company (LZ O2), which was commanded by Major Molloy. The remainder of the Battalion, including D Company (of Pegasus Bridge fame), were to land a matter of a few hundred yards

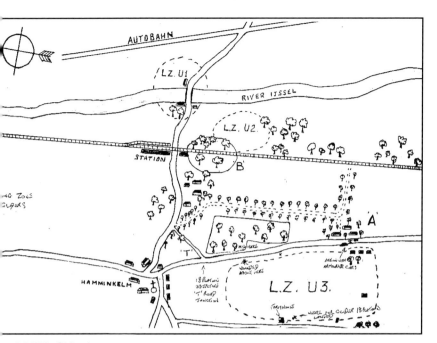

I RUR's Objective

6 Airlanding Brigade's Objectives and code letters.

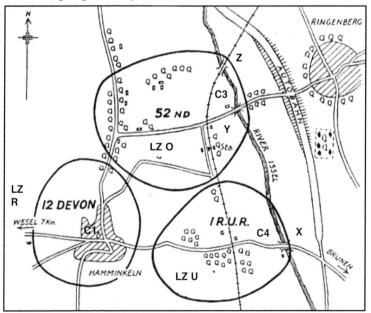

145

to the west, minutes later, on LZ O. According to the regimental historian:

> *It was known that the enemy had a small garrison at Hamminkeln and at Ringenburg who would probably guard the road bridges, and also that there was quite a number of light anti-aircraft guns on our landing zone. The enemy would probably try to counter-attack us, and it was possible that columns of reinforcements might be moving through the area as we landed.*

B and C Companies, born in four gliders each were all released successfully but glider No. 1 carrying 17 Platoon, B Company, piloted by Captain Carr received a direct hit from a heavy anti-aircraft gun at 2,000 feet and broke up, spilling men and equipment, with the loss of all aboard. In the second glider both Staff Sergeants Collins and Rowlands, were hit and wounded by AA fire and, consequently, the glider crashed into a wood east of the Issel, with about half of 18 Platoon loosing their lives. 19 Platoon's glider and that with B Company Headquarters landed just west of their bridge, which they stormed with sub-machine guns and grenades. The low quality German defenders of 84th Division, as at Pegasus Bridge, even without suffering the element of surprise, were no match for the ferocity of the attack. The fact

A sketch from the Illustrated London News of the Ox and Buck's LI's attack on the Issel Bridge. Note the sandbag built pill box on the enemy bank.

that they were manning their positions was probably negated by the preliminary bombardment.

C Company, commanded by Major Rahr, attacking the vital Ringenberg road bridge (Objective Y) had only one platoon and its HQ with which to capture it. Coming into land under fire from 20mm AA gun positions around Hamminkeln Station, 19 Platoon raced out of their glider, straight towards the bridge. A machine gun in a sandbag built pill box opened fire but having won the ensuing fire fight, the airborne soldiers closed in on the bridge using fire and manoeuvre. The road bridge was seized it before it could be blown.

No. 36 Grenade. Each glider infantryman carried two of these fragmentation grenades.

The Ox & Bucks LI's C Company, commanded by Major James Molloy, had better luck with his fly-in but his four glider's landing was more dispersed than anticipated. With his infantry force substantially intact, he advanced on the railway bridge, just as B Company, less than two hundred yards south, were attacking the road bridge. The outnumbered *volksgrenadiers* succumbed quickly to the determined Light Infantrymen and few escaped death or capture. At 1140 hours, Battalion Headquarters 2 Ox and Bucks LI was reporting to their Brigade HQ that both bridges had been captured and were now secure.

It is now considered highly likely that German commanders had not authorised the blowing of the Issel bridges, as their plans required them for both local counter-attacks by *Kampfgruppe Karst* and for those being planned by *XLVII Panzerkorps*. The engineers accompanying the Ox and Bucks's *coup de main* companies first made the bridges safe by cutting all existing enemy cables and fuses before working to prepare their own demolition charges and circuits for the bridges, in case they were in danger of falling into enemy hands.

1 RUR's battalion plan also called for D Company, under Major Tony Dyball, to mount a *coup de main* on the Hamminkeln-Brünen road bridge (Objective X). They were to land on LZ U1 and immediately seize the Issel Bridge. Major Charles Vickery's A Company was to land on LZ U2 and secure the buildings around the level crossing. The rest of the battalion would land on the main See sketch page 145 and map page 155

American Paratroopers pinned down on 6 Airlanding Brigade's LZ having been earlier mis-dropped.

LZ U3 and complete defensive positions covering the Issel to the west.

Major Dyball aboard the leading Horsa of D Company, landed heavily, at 1025, just 150 yards from the bridge. Several men were thrown through the Perspex cockpit canopy. Not only that, they were also promptly under *Spandau* fire from the bridge's garrison. Major Dyball and the conscious survivors of his Horsa's landing took cover from the *Spandau* in a gouge in the ground made by his aircraft's wing as it came to rest. He recalled that:

> *In a matter of seconds we had a Bren in action and it silenced the machine gun but another started up some thirty yards to its left. I could still see no sign of my other platoons. I decided I would make a dash across the open and get into a small wood and see if I could contact anyone there.*
>
> *The Bren covered me across and I contacted two glider pilots, two men from the Oxfordshire & Buckinghamshire Light Infantry and a few sappers. They had got into a good firing position covering the house that I wished to assault. I then moved the rest of my headquarters into a wood and we cleared it, killing two Germans. We then took up defensive positions. From where we were, a continuous trench ran up to the house and bridge. The Germans were still holding the house, although we could see a few retiring. A small party of enemy advanced towards us; we let them come until they were within twenty yards and then threw a 36 Grenade. Unfortunately it did not fall into the trench, though it exploded by its side. At once all hands went up. With two glider pilots and another two men, I went off down the trench towards the house. As we got to it, No 21 Platoon arrived from the other side of the road in fine form, having cleared the house and captured twenty-five prisoners. About another twenty-five were also rounded up.*
>
> *I then went across the bridge and found that No. 22 Platoon*

had done their job in clearing the houses. Although the platoon commander had been killed, the platoon sergeant, despite being wounded in the head, arm, leg and thigh, had led the platoon against strong opposition which was dug in. The bridge was in our hands and an all-round defence was quickly organised, consisting of four groups made up of the two platoons, Company Headquarters, some glider pilots, anti-tank gunners without their guns and a few men from the Oxfordshire & Buckinghamshire Light infantry. Although it was originally planned to capture the bridge with four platoons, this was the force which actually did so — some fifty men in total.

During the attack five German self-propelled guns came down the road [from the east]. *One was hit at twenty-five yards range by a PIAT but it was not knocked out. However, they showed no fight and retired as quickly as they could. About fifty prisoners were taken and about twenty Germans were killed."*

Meanwhile, only two A Company 1 RUR gliders landed on LZ U2. They brought in a pair of platoons commanded by Lieutenants John Stewart and Fred Laird. Deplaning, they headed off immediately but were under fire from 20mm guns near Hamminkeln. However, reaching their objectives, Ringenberg Station and the level crossing, there was little opposition. This area would appear to have already been dealt with by a mis-landed platoon of the 12 Devons, who were about a hundred yards west of

British tank stopper – the PIAT and its shaped charge warhead.

the railway, having captured fifty enemy troops who they found waiting quietly in a barn to surrender.

The Main Landing Zones

Coming in to the main LZ, Glider Pilot, Lieutenant Turner, in one of the last 6 Airlanding Brigade gliders, recalled that he '... could not see our own LZ or anybody else's' but eventually spotting the *autobahn* and identifying the Hamminkeln church he headed for LZ U.

> *Owing to the immediate vicinity being rather crowded with gliders we applied full flap, which results in a very steep dive and went down on the LZ as briefed. The five members of 1 RUR were none the worse after their unorthodox approach and proceeded to unload the Jeep and trailer containing petrol and ammunition. Suddenly there was a loud hissing and one of the [Horsa's] main wheels was hit. This stopped the unloading temporarily and we returned the fire. At this point we saw a Horsa in flames and when fifty feet from the ground the starboard main plane was blown off. The glider landed a little roughly, but the occupants were unhurt except for a few minor bruises.*

Flying Lieutenant Dennis Edwards's platoon of D Company Ox and Bucks LI, was RAF pilot Stan Jarvis in his damaged Horsa heading for LZ O. He wrote:

> *I could see the railway line and our objective, Hamminkeln Station, but enemy gunfire was becoming more accurate. I pulled out of the dive at about 50 feet above the ground then descended to almost ground level. We flew low over three fields, hitting post and wire fencing, which we were not aware existed, and were followed down the fields by a stream of tracer and incendiary bullets.*

Stan Jarvis's Horsa (RJ 246) was one of those aircraft flying into the area covered by the twelve 20mm light anti-aircraft guns that *Gefreiter* Herman Hagenberg and his comrades were manning. As RJ 246 came in to land its tail-unit was shot away, causing the glider to '... slew sideways close to the railway fence. Miraculously, none of the airborne troops was injured, for which I was very relieved.' Lieutenant Edwards of 2 Ox & Bucks recalled:

> *He put our Horsa down as close to the railway station as we could have wished. Many years later Stan told us how, after we had all*

fled the wrecked glider, taking cover wherever we could amid a hail of incoming missiles and bullets, one of the lads said to him, 'I know that before you left the airfield we asked you to get us as close as possible to the railway station, but if you had landed any closer we would have been in the ruddy booking office'.

The twenty-six-man platoon was lucky, as they all got clear of their glider and reached the station yard where they were forced to take refuge from the murderous German fire. The yard was stacked with piles of timber, each approximately the size of a two-storey house and covered a substantial area. Edwards recalled:

Unfortunately, it turned out that the Germans were using these stacks of timber to cover their approach as they advanced towards us. We spent the first few hours playing hide-and-seek among the wood-piles, dodging the German Mk IV tanks which trundled up and down the rows of stacked timber seeking us out.

We were not equipped to deal with German heavy tanks. Indeed, the anti-tank guns that we did possess, six-pounders could dispose of even a Tiger at close range, were almost certainly still within the Hamilcar gliders used to transport our heavier equipment. The concentration of enemy fire over the landing zones would have made it virtually impossible for such weapons to be removed. Most men were just thankful if they were able to crawl away from their gliders and find some sort of shelter from the

A view across the station to LZ O and Hamminkeln Windmill. Stan Jarvis's glider is just beyond the tree line. Note the damage to the starboard wing and lack of tail!

incoming German fire.

Stan Jarvis as a temporarily adopted member of Lieutenant Edwards's platoon was with them in the station yard:

> *Shortly after the landing a small group of German troops approached us from the direction of the River Issel, with a supporting light tank a tremendous firefight broke out with the airborne troops. A sergeant fired a PIAT shell at the tank which landed close to it, causing the driver and crew to quickly lose interest in us and it slewed round and rapidly withdrew with its supporting troops back towards the River Issel.*

According to Lieutenant Edwards his platoon was eventually forced out of the station yard by tanks firing at a long range from the east of the Issel.

Towards the end of the stream of gliders, HQ 6 Airlanding Brigade, Brigade troops and their security force, C Company 12 Devons, found that they were landing amongst almost an entire American parachute regiment, 513 PIR. They had been incorrectly dropped on LZ R, due to the smoke obscuring their DZ, which was

British and American paratroopers on LZ R.

just to the south and across the divisional boundary. They were in the act of moving off to their own area as the gliders swept in and the deplaning British were relieved to see that they had already dealt with many of the defenders. One Normandy veteran Swedebasher said 'Dead German and US troops lay all around the area of our RV. It was a nasty shock for some of the new lads to be suddenly projected into the midst of a battle'.

Private Taylor, also of 12 Devons, recalled the landing of subsequent waves on LZ R:

> *The next half hour was murderous; small arms and automatic fire from our own weapons added to the noise. I saw one of our gliders shot down with the loss of all on board, a four engine bomber flew across on fire, engines screaming, and obviously heading for a crash, and a heavy glider, one of our Hamilcars, came in low overhead and crashed straight into a railway signal box. It would seem impossible that anyone was left alive but although both of the pilots must have been killed, out of the wreckage came a small tank, intact and firing its machine guns. The boys inside must have landed already in their positions inside the tank and ready to fight. Other gliders were landing all around us and adding to the general confusion as they in turn opened fire.*

The landings on the main parts of LZs U and O were extremely chaotic, as not only were the Brigade landing through thick haze and smoke but also in the presence of the enemy; anti-aircraft gunners, in-place ground defences and, as the landings began, *Kampfgruppe Karst,* SS troops in the anti-airborne role. This battle group had a mix of armoured vehicles and, as intended at Arnhem, their tactical doctrine was 'to drive into the teeth of an airborne landing', doing as much damage as possible before the force could come together as a cohesive formation and require much greater combat power to contain or eliminate. Facing this type of challenge, immediately on arrival, is, of course, one of the reasons why airborne troops are specially selected for their resilience, independence and determination.

Not only were the troops of 6 Airlanding Brigade not prepared to be rolled over by the armour of *Kampfgruppe Karst* but the German's initial deployment had been east of the Issel where they had expected the Allied airborne landing. As the first parachutes blossomed to the west, their armoured columns immediately

This Panzer Mk IV has received a direct hit throughone of its road wheels.

started to cross the Issel into both the US and British areas and they were still crossing when the *coup de main* parties seized the bridges. Typhoon fighter bombers were also waiting in cab ranks to prevent enemy armour moving against the landing but it is believed that their rocket fire was ineffective due to the smoke, none the less they did help delay and disrupt a potentially dangerous threat. Consequently, even though they caused confusion and casualties on the LZs, *Kampfgruppe Karst* was unable to fight a coherent and decisive battle, not least because there were agressive airborne troops to be seen in every direction.

The counter-attacks by XLVII *Panzerkorps* were aimed either side of *Kampfgruppe Karst*. To the south, 116th *Windhund* Division attacked the Commando Brigade in Wesel and the American bridgehead, while 15th Panzer Grenadiers were active against 51st Highland Division to the north. In theory, the German's dispositions were excellent but they lacked combat power and above all air cover and support to be successful.

In the confusion on LZ R, about half of B Company 12 Devons, according to Lieutenant Allinson 'advanced in what they thought to be the right direction but after finding our position from a civilian, we returned to our original area and advanced on the twin spires of Hamminkeln.'

Typical of events on the LZ, were those that befell Rifleman Paddy O'Devlin, a pre-war regular Army soldier of 1 RUR, whose battle began immediately on landing in one of the minority of

A copy of the marked map accompanying the RUR's war diary.

undamaged gliders. Gripping his Bren gun, he was intent:

> ... *on getting out fast as soon as the glider landed and stopped. The two lads on either side of the door stood up and slid it into the roof and before anyone could move I was first out that door like a jackrabbit, jumped to the ground and ran to the tail of the glider to cover the rear as I had often done in training. As I ran I saw German soldiers in the two-storied farmhouse about 50 or 60 yards away, and one of them was firing a* Schmeisser *sub-*

machine gun in our direction. I threw myself down on the ground and shouldering my gun, brought it into the aim, at the same time releasing the safety catch. This only took seconds but the Germans nipped smartly back into the house. I put a few quick bursts after them through the door and windows to keep them pinned inside and not in a position to shoot us up, as the platoon got out of the glider.

I continued firing short bursts through the windows and doors, and as I was changing a magazine there was a shout that the Germans were running for Hamminkeln. I looked up and saw about a dozen of them from the house were legging it for cover behind a tall hedge away from us. In my excitement, I fired before I was properly into the aim and my burst hit the ground in front of me, I had to wait a few seconds before I could aim and fire again. This time I sprayed them as they were reaching the cover of the hedge and I could not say if I had hit any of them. … As I looked about at the platoon lying beside the glider everybody was flat on the ground, a ploughed field, taking cover, I seemed to be the only one firing.

Then there was a shout that two German tanks [Kg Karst] were coming up the road. This road ran north-south … about seventy yards or so away. I repositioned my Bren gun so that I could fire at them as they came opposite the glider …. In the event they weren't tanks but armoured personnel half track vehicles. In the first one, the Germans were standing up, shoulder to shoulder; they had obviously packed it as much as possible. … As they came opposite I let them have a burst and they all collapsed behind the armoured sides, I couldn't have hit them all but there was an amount of shouting and screaming. The troops in the second vehicle were concealed behind the armour, having no doubt seen what happened to the first vehicle, they were travelling about 50 yards behind but I sprayed it with a burst anyway, hoping to hit the driver. Both vehicles continued on towards Hamminkeln. I was highly elated, my attitude was that I'd got some of the bastards before they got me.

For some considerable time Rifleman O'Devlin's platoon, No 18, without its commander, did not make any attempt to cross LZ U3 to their objective, a 'T' road junction south of Hamminkeln, due to the volume of small arms fire. Returning the fire, O'Devlins Bren gun eventually jammed when it overheated. It became apparent, however, that the enemy fire was principally at the gliders rather than at them and despite the temptation to:

... lie doggo, I knew it was time we got a move on. ... so I called out to our platoon sergeant, Geordie, lets get to the objective. He immediately shouted, at No. 2 Section 'get to the objective'. At that, they picked themselves up and away they went at the double and I followed. I ran, with my Bren gun in my right hand, holding the carrying handle on the barrel, which was too hot to hold. Under my left arm, I had a pile of empty magazines, which I intended to reload at the objective. When we were about halfway there and still in the ploughed field, the empty magazines slipped from my arm and fell on the ground so I stopped to pick them up. As I ran on again, I realised I was now running alone. Passing a couple of dead airborne, made me decide to alter my direction and make directly for the ditch at the side of the road, under cover of which, I could make my way to the road junction. I suddenly noticed two Germans working on a Spandau *machine gun. They were at the edge of the wood on the far side of the road and I expect their gun was jammed and I knew I had to get to the ditch before they cleared it. Whilst still about 20 yards from the ditch and possibly 80 yards from the Germans they got behind the* Spandau *and started to feed a belt into it. As I was the only one in view, up and running directly towards them I was their target. It flashed through my mind to zigzag but I must have turned to zig when, I was hit. Instead of getting a burst in the stomach I had turned out of the line*

SS troops setting up an MG-42 on its sustained fire tripod mounting.

of fire and was hit in the right fore arm below my elbow breaking the bone. When I was hit I was thrown forward, letting a shout of 'Oh' and fell flat on my face with my arms in front of me to protect my head. It all happened automatically and I lay there for some seconds before I knew I was hit and did not move. They did not fire again and I found I could not move which was just as well for me, as I might have attracted more fire from them and I had a small anti-tank mine tied on the strap of my small pack on my back, if they hit it I'd be blown to pieces.

Paddy O'Devlin was eventually pulled off the LZ into a ditch by the epaulettes of his airborne smock. Small actions like this against *Kampfgruppe Karst* were taking place all over the battlefield and in many cases, they prevented more than a small fraction of the number of men planned, from being able to attack their objectives. Brigadier Bellamy wrote, however:

> ... *sufficient troops of each battalion were landed in the correct places, and most important of all, a percentage of the* coup-de-main *parties landed by the bridges. All-important objectives were either in out hands or neutralised and ready for plucking by 1130 hours.*

1 RUR duly reported that it was, in position south-east of Hamminkeln and the Ox and Bucks were reporting that although they were in position, they numbered only two hundred men and were under mounting pressure. It was, however, expected that seizing, clearing and holding the village of Hamminkeln itself would take longer. Brigadier Bellamy stated that throughout the battle on the LZs '... ground opposition was stronger than anticipated, every farmhouse was a strong point and there were a considerable number of SP guns and half tracks milling around the Brigade area'.

Rifleman Paddy O'Devlin was by now on his way back to the Regimental Aid Post, which was in a house with a crashed glider completely blocking the road.

> ... *as we reached the glider someone shouted 'Tanks' at which my two helpers took off and left me. I realised the tanks were coming along the road on the far side of the glider and I shuffled my way to the ditch and let myself slide in and crouched against the bank and partially concealed by the glider. ... The' tanks', which were travelling about 100 yards apart, turned out to be eight wheel armoured cars and they had wounded soldiers on top trying to reach their own forces by way of Hamminkeln. The first one tried to smash its way at speed through the glider but the driver lost control and it finished up in the ditch beyond me about 20 yards away. As its commander climbed out of the turret, I saw a burst of bullets hit his helmet and he flopped over. The second car tried to lever his way through the glider and then all hell*

Sd Kfz 234/2 Puma heavy armoured car

158

broke lose when our lads opened up with Bren guns and a 6-pounder anti-tank gun setting it on fire.

Elsewhere, parties of Swedebashers who should have been clearing Hamminkeln (see Chapter 9) became caught up in similar engagements. An NCO was being shot at from a windmill and closing in on it, posted grenades through doors and windows and was surprised when forty Germans came out to surrender. Elsewhere, A Company's HQ, consisting of company commander – Captain Carey, Sergeant Major and runner, took on a pair of *Kampfgruppe Karst*'s tanks (probably SP assault guns) and a pair of SdkFz-251 Hannomag half-tracks.

The Glider Pilots

The glider pilots, including attached RAF personnel, having delivered their cargo of troops, were now themselves' combat troops and expected to make themselves useful. Lieutenant Harrington, who had piloted one of fourteen Horsas flying out of RAF Gosfield, had managed to land within fifty yards of his objective; a farmhouse. His de-briefer wrote:

The farmhouse was occupied by German soldiers whose equipment included an 88mm gun. As soon as the glider landed, the Germans turned everything on the Glider, the troops in the glider could not get out as the hatches had jammed and a number

Prisoners of war being marched to the divisional cage, escorted by glider pilots.

were killed by the Germans' fire. Those who finally got out by chopping their way through the side of the glider occupied a slit trench with only one rifle and one revolver as their defending armament.

The S/Ldr GPR was in a similar situation not far away. Also not far away was a German emplacement containing Oelikon guns. The S/Ldr, getting a little fed up with the situation, stood on the edge of the trench and shouted to the Germans …
'Come out you German Bastards and fight out here'.
The Germans immediately put their hands up and surrendered.

Lieutenant Harrington, with the help of some mis-dropped American paratroopers duly cleared the farm house.

Having landed a platoon of D Company 2 Oxs & Bucks and taken part in his first battle, Stan Jarvis made his way to his Squadron's RV:

After the airborne troops overran Hamminkein station it was necessary for my co-pilot and myself to leave the soldiers and to work our way up the railway track to a pre-planned rendezvous point. The pilots were not regarded as combat troops after the initial fighting had ceased.

The glider pilots' were to establish a PW cage and to properly search German prisoners for items of intelligence value. Stan Jarvis was one of the searchers and continues his account:

Personal items, such as photographs, letters and non-military items, were returned to the prisoner. I was personally directed to search prisoners in a large room, about 25 feet square. The German troops were facing the walls all the way round the room with their hands up. I started to search each prisoner whilst another pilot covered them with a Sten gun. After a time I realised that an enormous amount of Dutch Guilders were accumulating on a table which I had been given for the purpose. Bundles of bank notes were being removed from prisoners' pockets, amounting to thousands. A couple of prisoners who could speak English, admitted sheepishly that their unit had been withdrawn across the Rhine and they had ransacked a bank before leaving.

In a lighter vein, I searched a young prisoner – about my own age – and removed a handful of contraceptives from his tunic pocket. I requested his English speaking comrades to tell him that it would be a long time before he would be able to use them. The other enemy troops roared with laughter when it was explained in German.

When the number of prisoners became too high for us to house, we marched them all to the village of Hamminkeln which had been captured by the Devon Regiment, which landed next to the village.

Another glider pilot recalled:

Whilst dealing with German prisoners, I was with a prisoner who spoke perfect English and asserted that "You were late weren't you!" I was rather miffed ... "We expected you at 10 A.M. but you arrived at 10 minutes past 10 A.M." So much for security!

Lieutenant Turner recalled that airmen always like their comforts and that three hours after the landing '...there was a pleasant smell of bacon and eggs from Sqn HQ, a *Wehrmacht* stores by the level crossing east of Hamminkeln'. Later, at about 1800hrs the glider pilots were allocated front line defensive positions as part of 6th Airborne Division's perimeter.

The Airborne Armour Arrives

At 1050 hours, Lieutenant Colonel Stewart aboard the Hamilcar, with a T9E1 Locust light tank aboard, was cast off from their tug aircraft. Trooper Dowset recalled:

The guns were loaded, the engine started and we were all set. I heard one of the glider pilots say, 'Hang on, chaps. We're going in now.' A very short time later we seemed to be going around and around and then an almighty crash, we came to halt upside down suspended by our safety harnesses.

A Carrier of the Air Landing Brigade by its Hamilcar glider.

A Locust being loaded into a Hamilcar glider.

The Hamilcar had lost a part of its wing to a light anti-aircraft battery and duly crashed. Eventually, getting themselves free, Dowset and the two other crew members were surprised to see the CO's tank that landed very wide of LZ P motoring up on the way the RV. 'The Commanding Officer himself, bedecked in his brightly coloured cavalry forage cap, was sounding his hunting horn as he stood upright in the turret!' The regimental war diary recorded, '*En route* to the RV the CO picked up one more tank which had gone through a house, a runner but guns out of action'.

The arrival at the RV of the four of the eight T9E1 Locust light tanks of 6th Airborne Armoured Recce Regiment, immediately helped matters on the LZ considerably. The Recce Regiment's war diarist wrote:

> *The rear link light tank (Lt Kenward) landed OK in the right area and was in action immediately, only to be brewed up by an 88-mm while supporting Americans who were clearing up a farm building. Of the remainder, one (Sgt Dawson) was reported to have been shot out of the air and another damaged* en

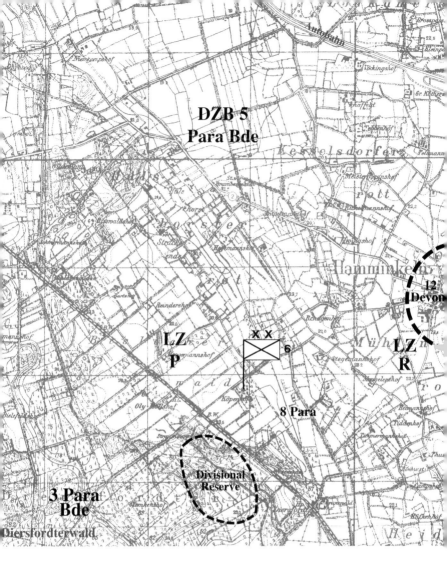

route *to the RV, remained in action* [as a pill-box] *all day in front of 12 Para Battalion's positions. Four tanks eventually reached the RV and occupied the high feature 1847 south of Kopenhof and the railway embankment.*

The Locusts came under fire almost immediately and were allocated a platoon of C Company 12 Devons to support them.

During the ensuing fight, casualties were suffered both by ourselves and the Devons, one Troop Sergeant being wounded and

A modified 6-pounder belonging to the Air Landing Brigade is starting to be dug-in by its crew. The spire of Hamminkeln church can be seen in the background.

the infantry platoon commander being killed, both forward tanks were hit by MMGs and were fired on by heavier guns. During the night, all tanks were moved into section areas, and the sections themselves reinforced with Glider Pilots.

The same enemy groups that were confronting 8 Para in the Dieserfordterwald were active against the Armoured Recce Regiment, attempting to infiltrate into their position. They were dealt with by machine gun and small arms fire and withdrew before dawn.

Logistics

Coming in immediately after the landing was a daring, low-level re-supply sortie flown by 240 American Liberator bombers, which delivered 540 tons of petrol, food and ammunition. This was necessary as the airborne divisions could only drop with sufficient combat supplies for their immediate needs and Second Army would not be in position to replenish them, even if all went well until, D+1. Fourteen of the four-engined aircraft were shot down and many more damaged but fortunately, about 85 percent of their containers were accurately dropped and recovered.

Not only had medics dropped with the parachute brigades and landed with the glider troops but as Corporal Cooper recalled a substantial medical facility was flown into LZ P. He reported:

> The initial casualties had been fairly heavy, first count revealed a loss of 40% of the brigade, but a number had been taken prisoner, only to be released after a brief period and able to rejoin their units. Of the 13 gliders carrying 195 Field Ambulance personnel, one came down in Holland, one with 15 personnel was captured as it landed, but were released by the Americans… and a third carrying 25 personnel was also captured…
>
> The work on the Main Dressing Station was hectic, and by midnight, a seven hundred bed hospital was fully operative. In addition to the blankets carried by the unit; additional supplies were scrounged from the locals. Apart from these duties, I had been occupied as a stretcher-bearer, and as the wards were on the upper floors, this was heavy work. At midnight half the unit was stood down and I was able to get some sleep till 06:00, at this time I had to complete a state of unit report for Divisional Headquarters.

Trenches were soon dug in the sandy soil for protection against motors and artillery. A dressing station with casualties awaiting evacuation.

Consolidation

By 1300 hours, the battle on and around the LZs was all but over. Patrols for the remainder of the day were rounding up remaining Germans who were mostly either lying up or attempting to escape. This gave 6th Airlanding Brigade the opportunity to dig-in for the expected counter-attacks. The one thing that gave Brigadier Bellamy concern was the increasing pressure from the north being exerted by *7th Fallschirmjäger,* who unlike the luckless 84th Volksgrenadierdivision, had been spared the worst of the airborne onslaught.

> *The only cohesive enemy force in the area was reported in Ringenburg during the late afternoon and evening, and included a small number of tanks. 2 Ox & Bucks was too reduced in numbers to be able to deal with it, but medium artillery and RAF Typhoons attacked it, and they caused no further trouble.*

The leading elements of 6th Airborne Division's land-tail crossed the Rhine by Buffalo and reached their parent units by 1830 hours. These were principally personnel and light vehicles and equipment rather than a significant quantity of stores.

Prisoners grouped into batches of twenty to be transported to the west bank of the Rhine.

CHAPTER NINE

12 Devons at Hamminkeln

Hamminkeln is a large straggling village in the centre of 6th Airborne Division's area, which, if held by the enemy, would have formed a bastion from which they could dominate a large part of ground, as well as denying an important road hub. Failure to capture it promptly would mean a protracted battle or, as in the case of Wesel, consume numerous troops to overcome the defenders. This made Hamminkeln the Brigade's most important objective and its capture was allocated to the 'Sweedbashers'.

Brigadier Bellamy described his intentions for the three companies available to Lieutenant Colonel Paul Gleadell:

> *12 Devons were to land west of Hamminkeln* [LZ R]: *the Battalion was to first seal off the place from the north, west and south* [phase 1] *and then attack and capture it* [phase 2]. *This battalion only had three companies, as one* [C Company] *had to be detached for duty with divisional HQ.*

In more detail the Devon's CO, Lieutenant Colonel Gleadell, recounted how in Phase 1:

> *D Coy, with the Anti-Tank P1 (less two detachments) and some pioneers, was the coup-de-main Company. It was to land as close into the village on the west side as possible, seize the Western Crossroads ...* [in Hamminkeln], *and exploit to the road junctions* [just to the east and north of this position].
>
> *A Coy, with one anti-tank platoon, was to land south-west and south of Hamminkeln and isolate the objective from the south and south-west.*
>
> *B Coy, with two 17-pounders, was to land west of the objective and isolate Hamminkeln from the north and north-west.*
>
> *The Reconnaissance Platoon was to land with B Coy and patrol to the large copse where they were to liaise with 1 RUR and prevent infiltration between the copse and Hamminkeln.*

The MMG Platoon were to cover the entrances north and south of

167

A Glider in its final approach to its LZ.

Hamminkeln, while the Mortar Platoon was to be prepared to give local fire support, despite the general ban on artillery fire support during the landing period.

Phase 2 was to begin immediately Hamminkeln was isolated and the battalion were free to concentrate on entering the village.

D Coy was to clear the centre of the village and be responsible for the defence of the objective to the east and south-east. A Coy was to clear and hold the South of the village, and B Coy was to assault and hold the North-East and North-West face of the village. C Coy when available was to concentrate in reserve at the houses 181486 [a mile west of Hamminkeln] *and be prepared to counter-attack the objective. Roadblocks were to be erected and manned on all approaches.*

Colonel Gleadell landed on the Ox and Bucks LI's LZ amidst a battle between a platoon of that regiment and the enemy in Ringenburg. After some Germans left a nearby copse surrendered, the Colonel realised that he had been incorrectly landed on the banks of the Issel near the railway bridge. Heading south along the railway track with his Tactical HQ, including a soldier who had been wounded by ground fire during the landing; his group arrived at the correct LZ. He wrote:

The whole situation was chaotic, and I wondered if we should ever get it unravelled. Every farmhouse appeared to contain a defended post and isolated battles were being fought out by detached parties all over the LZ and beyond.

However, the chaos was not entirely one-sided. Colonel Gleadell continued:

The enemy were in greater confusion than we were. A number managed to concentrate in Hamminkeln, particularly on the north-east side. They consisted mostly of flak gunners, Luftwaffe Regiment, Volksturm *and Parachutists. Three SP guns, some tanks, armoured cars and half-tracks were cruising about the LZ and engaged troops who were de-planing.*

The area was covered with light flak gun positions, manned mainly by personnel of Battle Group Karst. This was a special anti-airlanding formation with small groups of men, mostly paratroops, or Waffen SS, *in various places throughout the 84 Div area. The Germans had evidently appreciated the likelihood of an airborne operation in this area.*

The CO, however, was not the only man struggling to make sense of the chaos. Lieutenant Bill Cotton of D Company was one of many who had landed with bullets cracking about him, and had, along with his platoon, taken cover in a ditch and set about working out where they were. Corporal Anderson recalled that 'with no landmarks visible, it was an impossible task' from their position in the ditch.

Corporal Anderson.

Telling us to stay where we were, Bill Collins crawled to the top of the embankment with his map and binoculars. Then he committed a brave but suicidal act by standing up to get a better view. He was immediately hit and fell face downwards, with his body lying at an unnatural angle on the top of the bank. I did not have to risk my life to see whether his pulse was still beating. He was lying in one of those grotesque positions only assumed by the dead.

Making their way towards their objective, the remains of the platoon gathered other groups of men as they went but they came across no officers or senior NCOs. Eventually arriving north of the village, Corporal Anderson and his followers met a further body of men from other gliders, but again no sergeants. However, a moment later two men came rolling down the bank with a burst of

Spandau fire kicking up the dirt. They were Colonel and his batman.

> 'Who's in charge here?' demanded the Colonel, struggling to his feet. Nobody answered. 'Speak up, someone,' barked the Colonel.
>
> 'I don't know whether I'm the senior NCO, sir,' I said, 'but our platoon commander has been killed, and the platoon sergeant has been cut off, and we've no maps.'
>
> 'Who are you, then?' asked the Colonel.
>
> 'Corporal Anderson, 31 Platoon, D Company, sir.'
>
> 'Right, then,' the Colonel was spreading out his map. 'This is where we are now. I believe your objective is the southern end of the town, about a mile up the road,' and he pointed to the location on his map. I nodded agreement. 'We can't wait for any more men,' continued the Colonel. 'We'll probably be joined by a few stragglers on the way, and we'll just have to manage with what we've got.'

Private Taylor, whose platoon was already advancing on Hamminkeln, also provides an account of action on the DZ and his meeting with the CO:

> We had landed about half a mile from the town, but managed to locate it through the smoke and haze. The platoon commander ordered us to move off in that direction. Some three hundred yards or so from the town we became pinned down by heavy small arms fire and began taking quite a number of casualties. In one section near to me Bert and Frank had been wounded and Stevenson killed, and I believe there were more casualties in other sections. The platoon commander called for smoke, and I reminded him of

Airbourne soldiers piling around a Jeep and trailor.

the Brigadier's request, but before he could reply we were joined by
the Colonel who quickly took command of the situation. He
obviously knew where we were and what our objective was.

Colonel Gledell, against orders, was wearing his red beret rather than his steel helmet and was fighting the battle in shirtsleeves, with his batman carrying his smock and battledress jacket. He eventually managed to get through to Main Battalion HQ and B Company on the radio and ascertaining that his rifle companies were establishing 'an admittedly thin cordon around Hamminkeln'. He gave the order for phase 2 and later recalled that:

> *... I myself joined up with a platoon of D Company and we*
> *concentrated about the road junction north of the village and, after*
> *encountering some resistance, reached the northern edge of*
> *Hamminkeln.*

Corporal Anderson's account of these events is, however, altogether more revealing:

> *By the time we were ready to move, more men had joined us, and*
> *we now mustered nearly fifty, to capture the town of Hamminkeln*
> *with its vital road junctions; an undertaking for which our*
> *planners had allocated five hundred men. But I got the impression*
> *that our determined colonel was quite prepared to attempt it,*
> *single-handed if necessary.*
>
> *The Germans had snipers covering almost every section of the*
> *elevated roadway. However, there were houses that might offer*
> *cover at intervals of about two hundred yards or so along the road.*
> *So the Colonel told us to leap-frog from one to another, spacing*
> *ourselves from five to ten yards apart, running like hares and only*
> *regrouping when we arrived at the outskirts of the town.*

With the Colonel leading and his batman following, Corporal Anderson led the soldiers of D Company towards the outskirts of the village. With the words '... for God's sake don't stop running till you're under cover. Best of luck, see you in Hamminkeln.' he was off, followed a second or so later by his batman'. Private Taylor commented:

> *His fearless attitude and personal bravery instilled courage into*
> *all of those present, and we were so inspired by him that when he*
> *shouted 'follow me' and dashed away, all of us were up and behind*
> *him to a man. I was the first man next to him, and we ran, then*

> *crawled, then ran again toward the town.*
>
> *My friend Tom Gittings was hit and doubled up lying over a barbed wire fence. I thought he had been killed but I had no time to stop; it was not until some months later that I found he was still alive.*

Before following, Corporal Anderson yelled to his section:

> *All get up from the bank in different places when your turn comes. If you all take the same route, Jerry will draw a bead on that position, and you'll have had it. The ones I could see nodded. "OK. Let's go," I yelled, and I scrambled up the bank.*

Reaching the first house, the Swedebashers kicked the doors in'... hoping to God the Jerries have only got small arms and that there aren't any tanks or artillery to shell the houses'. Colonel Gledeall commented that 'The capture of Hamminkeln was to begin at 1135 hours. The companies duly assaulted the village and the objective was taken by midday'. Once again this simple statement belies the difficulties of the break in battle and reaching their objectives in the village centre.

Under fire from unseen riflemen in the houses of Hamminkeln, this is where fitness counted. Anderson had cause to thank his 'running prowess, improved by all those cross-country runs, which served me well'. He dived through a gap in a hedge, wriggled on his stomach to the door and moved quickly inside. Having equally quickly cleared the house his section were preparing for their next dash:

> *The Colonel was already knocking out the window frame on the opposite side of the house. Through the window he climbed and was off on the next lap of his mad journey. The batman and I followed. Behind me I could hear footsteps and hoped that the rest of the platoon were still coming on, but there was no time even to turn my head to see as it was a good two hundred yards, probably more, to the next house, which occupied a bend in the road. Wherever the German snipers were, they had evidently realized that the long gap between the two houses was going to be their best opportunity and concentrated their fire about ten yards from the house which was our objective. The Colonel made it safely, but his batman went down about ten yards from safety.*

Anderson was nearly hit by small arms fire. There were two cracks, as one bullet whizzed past his ankles and another uncomfortably near to his head, which 'provided adrenalin' for him to continue moving at top speed. The soldier immediately behind him, went down with a single bullet wound. With every second being vital, the killed and wounded had to be left.

Writing almost sixty years after the event, Private Taylor also recalled the horror of that gap.

There was a gap between a house and a wall which was a death trap to those who were not quick enough to cross it. It was the last twenty yards of a long exhausting run under fire that were most dangerous. It was only natural that one would slow down at the end of that run just when safety was in sight, but enemy snipers overlooked the spot, and caused a lot of casualties. Each man that got across safely stayed there in turn to warn and urge speed from the next man across. The snipers were hidden in the church spire which I had seen in the model at the time of our briefing. Our return small arms fire did not seem to have any effect, and they continued to cause havoc and heavy casualties for quite a while.

The battle became confused and the house clearing drills learned in the abandoned villages of Salisbury Plain and the blitzed parts of Southampton, came to the fore. Corporal Anderson recounted:

An SS Sniper with his K98 rifle with an optic scope.

The Colonel advanced to the first doorway, while my men and I, with our backs to the wall on the other side of the road, covered every doorway and window on his side. When he was safely in position, it was our turn to advance, while he covered us. So, doorway by doorway, house by house, we crept forward.

Suddenly, machine gun fire spurted from an upstairs window just ahead. I burst open the front door of the next house on our side, closely followed by two men. They ran upstairs and began firing at the house from which the firing had come, while I, at a ground-floor window, pointed it out to the Colonel. Keeping close to the wall, he took three men forward, inching along with their backs to the wall. When they arrived at the manned house, on which we were keeping up a constant fire, they tossed grenades through the front door. Just to make sure, one of the men dashed to

Enemy and Airbourne soldiers awaiting and receiving treatment during the Operation VARSITY D-Day.

the middle of the road, lobbed a grenade into the upstairs window and leaped back to cover again. As soon as the grenades had exploded, the three men ran into the house. I heard a rattle of gunfire from inside and then the men emerged, covered with dust but unhurt …

Presently, Anderson reached the first crossroads that was D Company's original objective and recognized, from the large scale aerial photographs he had been shown during briefing, the main square of Hamminkeln. The square was dominated by a large building over which a swastika was flying, but as it had not been one of his original objectives he wasn't sure what it was. He explained how 'Corporal', shouted the Colonel from across the road, 'that's the anti-aircraft headquarters. Take your section and clear it while I carry on through the town'.

Taking the first seven men of my section, I dashed across to the building and tossed grenades in at the ground and first floors. We did not risk throwing any at the upper floors in case we missed and they rebounded on us. We flattened ourselves against the outside walls of the buildings until the grenades exploded; then in we went. We found that the house had a central staircase. Telling Harry Harris and Ray Best to clear the ground floor, I started up the stairs, followed by the others. At the first floor, I left behind Jack Nichols and Ted Lockey, to clear that level; at the second, Tombstone and Jakoff That left Ponsonby and myself to deal with the attic. Frank followed me up the narrow stairway, ready for anything, but the birds had flown. Only their commander remained, and as I burst into the attic, I was confronted by a German SS captain, who saluted and handed me his Walther automatic pistol, butt first.

It took ten minutes to clear the building 'or rather to search it to make sure there were no lurking enemy'. The enemy had obviously gone leaving an officer to operate the radio up until the last possible moment. During the searching Anderson found some mementos of Hamminkeln.

I then went quickly through the contents of the attic and found a Schmeisser *sub-machine carbine and dagger, with the SS insignia and swastika on it, and this I tucked inside my belt. Finally, I pulled down the German flag from the roof and stowed it inside my airborne-smock. It would make a splendid souvenir.*

A wounded German prisoner is questioned as a guard looks on.

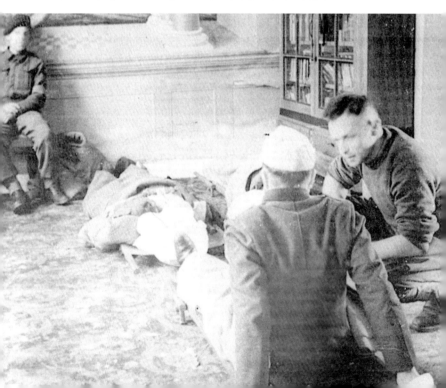

The tension of battle is obvious from this confrontation with Brigadier Bellamy (left) and Major Eddie Warren during the reorganisation phase in Hamminkeln.

Private Taylor also recalled reaching the centre of the village.

> *We rushed the enemy still ensconced in a few houses and captured our objective, the crossroads. About one hundred enemy soldiers surrendered to us there, a mixture of young and old, Home Guard and regular soldiers; we disarmed them and shoved them in to a hall of sorts, I think it was the school. We would not have made it*

A 12 Devons 6-pounder anti-tank gun crew pose for the official photograph in Hamminkeln. The proper gun pit was still being dug behind the gun.

but for the CO.

> He had disappeared, and we found out soon after that he had gone to find the 6-pounder antitank platoon, and having done so, used them to blow those enemy snipers in the church steeple to kingdom come.

> Suddenly the noise of battle ceased; it seemed just as if someone had waved a baton like an orchestra conductor at the end of a concert. One moment it was very loud and noisy, and the next moment, silence. The battle was over. I looked at my watch. It had taken only one hour and twenty minutes from landing to finish, but it seemed as if we had been fighting for hours, such a lot of action had taken place in that short period of time. We were cockahoop now that it was over, and feeling on top of the world at the success of the operation.

Returning to the square, Corporal Anderson recalled 'No one fired at us, and, indeed, there was no sound of gunfire in the town at all, only the distant noise of battle and the Swedebashers were, in control of their objective. They had done what they had been ordered to do, but with about one-tenth of the number of men, the planners had calculated they would need. As Anderson said, 'It was yet another case of well trained men under inspired leadership achieving the seemingly impossible'.

German prisoners including members of assault gun crews are marched out of Hamminkeln. RAF glider pilot Stan Jarvis is to the right of the prisoners wearing a beret.

A victory, however, is not complete and can prove to be a temporary state of affairs, if soldiers rest on their laurels. Colonel Gleadell led the consolidation and mopping-up, which was 'vigorously carried out in anticipation of the expected counter-attack and to eliminate the remaining flak positions'.

Colonel Gleadell paid tribute to the Army and Royal Air Force glider pilots 'Who throughout this period did invaluable work under Major Priest, in rounding up and controlling the very considerable number of prisoners (approximately) 500 in the Battalion area'.

12 Devon's casualties during the morning were:

	Officers	ORs	Total
Killed	6	24	30 (out of 700)
Wounded	5	25	30 (all evacuated)
Missing	5	75	80 (50 later found to be killed)
	16	124	140

'For his part, the enemy casualties must have been heavy during the day.'

With the town taken and mopping up complete, 12 Devons prepared defensive positions in and around Hamminkeln and became the Brigade's reserve.

A Devon's carrier prepares to patrol the streets of Hamminkeln in order to dominate the area.

CHAPTER TEN

Link up and Breakout

By 1130 on 24 March 1945, most of 6th Airborne Division's important objectives had been seized and between 1300 and 1500 hours, the three brigades reported that they were in place on their objectives or defensive positions and digging-in. Their battle was, however, far from over. They had in effect superimposed themselves on top of the enemy's defences. Although they had effectively subdued most organized opposition plenty of enemy soldiers were still in the Divisional area. They had also taken up positions sandwiching the remains of *84th Volksgrenadier Division* between them and the advancing 15th Scottish Division, with whom substantive contact was yet to be made. They were also in possession of crossings of the River Issel, vital to both the defence by 6th Airborne Division and to German counter-attacks.

The two parachute brigades were digging-in; 3 Parachute Brigade in the Dieserfordterwald around Bergfurth and 5 Parachute Brigade north-east of the forest and across the railway line, while 6 Airlanding Brigade was preparing to defend the Issel bridges and the village of Hamminkeln. The latter village was a significant feature in the Divisional layout and Colonel Gledell's 12 Devons were establishing a strong point in its substantial buildings. Major General Bols intended that Hamminkeln would be 'a pivotal point in the Division's scheme of defence, that an enemy counter-attack, which had successfully crossed the Issel, would find hard to overcome'.

Having fought with the infantry during the landing phase the glider pilots were now concentrated into their squadrons and running the brigades' and Divisional PW cages, but now the initial rush of prisoners was subsiding and with most of the Germans seemingly content to be out of the war, some glider pilots were released to prepare additional defences in the Airlanding Brigade perimeter, against the inevitable German counter-attacks. The Glider Pilot Squadrons, however, continued to be responsible for the prisoners who were to be held east of the Rhine for some days, as, initially, there was a strict one-way (forward only) policy on the bridges that the Royal Engineers were to establish across the Rhine.

3 Para Brigade

Brigadier Hill's plan was for his brigade to dominate the Dieserfordterwald with aggressive patrols, covering gaps and identifying enemy attempting to advance or infiltrating through their part of the Divisional area. They were also manning pre-arranged contact points on the Wesel-Emmerich road where they would meet members of 507 PIR and to their west where they would link up with 15th Scottish Division.

Shortly after midday, DZ A was finally cleared and, while moving into brigade reserve, 8 Para encountered a pair of 88 mm guns in the Dieserforderwald. These guns fired high explosive shells into the trees, as the paras approached. The effect of the bursting shells was enhanced by numerous splinters of wood that caused nasty wounds, which were difficult to treat and in previous wars would have had led to a very high mortality rate. However, penicillin now greatly enhanced survival rates.

The nature of the patrol actions that developed from midday into the night differed widely. In some places it was a question of rounding up stray Germans, in others ambushing or indeed being ambushed. Others fought off organised groups of enemy, of up to platoon strength, who clearly intended to fight their way back

Royal Engineers established light and heavy ferries across the Rhine on 24 March.

A 44 Lowland Brigade armoured car brought 15th Scottish Division officers forward to make the link with the Airborne.

across the Issel. In these circumstances, casualties mounted and, for example, a group of 8 Para, including a liaison officer and the Padre, who were on their way to visit the wounded at 224 Field Ambulance, located in the nearby houses in the hamlet of Bergfurth, were ambushed and killed.

A little further to the north in the same wood, 1 Canadian Para were sending out clearance patrols:

> ... *Sergeant A. Page took out a six-man patrol to reconnoitre the woods in the vicinity of the company's positions. He returned a short while later, escorting nearly a hundred prisoners who were promptly added to those already captured.*

During the afternoon, it was reported that C Company's 5 Platoon, who had been left on the DZ had suffered very heavy casualties, when *Fallschirmjäger* pushed forward from the hamlet of Höfges and that Lieutenant Brunnette, the platoon commander, was reported to have been killed. Nevertheless:

> *C Company consolidated its defences* [in the Dieserfordterwald] *and proceeded to bring effective fire to bear on numbers of enemy*

troops who were moving around the company's area. By mid-afternoon the situation had quietened down and the area seemed clear of the enemy.

Later in the day, the enemy counter-attacked in an effort to recapture the area but they were beaten off. A heavy mortar concentration was then brought down on A Company's position, followed by a large enemy patrol moving up. This attack was also beaten off, with several enemy being taken prisoner.

The all-important link up with the leading elements of 15th Scottish Division was made at 1400 hours, at the small bridge to the west of the Dieserfordterwald known as 'Alpha'. The first unit to reach 3 Para Brigade was 8 Royal Scots, while patrols from 6 Kings Own Scottish Boarder met 9 Para patrols a little further south. To avoid fratricide, the recognition signal to prevent exchanges of friendly fire was the '… waving yellow cleanse triangles, carried by all ranks of the brigade groups who cross on D Day'. Brigadier Poett commented that 'In addition, red berets were to be worn after the initial drop'. Finally, a radio contact channel (No.38) had also been established to manage this most dangerous of situations, where two friendly forces approach each other during the height of a battle in order to link-up. At 1545 hours, Commander 44 (Lowland) Infantry Brigade and the Commanding Officer of 8 Royal Scots arrived at HQ 3 Para Brigade, met Brigadier Hill and 'were given a rousing reception by the parachutists'.

HQ 6th Airbourne Division was dug-in at Kopenhof.

Divisional Headquarters

Divisional HQ and the Artillery Group HQ, with C Company of 12 Devons to protect it, had landed in gliders on DZ P and set up at Kopenhof. At 1100 hours they reported having established communications with the two para brigades but it took a further 28 minutes to raise 6 Airlanding Brigade, who were of course locked in battle with *Kampfgruppe Karst*. Rear link communications were established with XVIII US at 1335 hours. Meanwhile, individual FOU parties had been speaking to their guns west of the Rhine almost immediately and HQ RA 6th Airborne was running a support net to coordinate artillery fire and air support across the Division.

As dusk fell, despite patrols from the three brigades combing the woods, farms and villages, the enemy, many of whom had been lying-up until dark, became more active, either with aggressive intent or simply trying to exfiltrate to their own lines under the cover of darkness. Either way, the number of Germans in the wood and making their way around Divisional HQ was becoming a severe nuisance and:

> ...REAR Div HQ, in a farm WEST of the railway, about half a mile away was subject to sniping and mortaring from woods to the WEST during most of the afternoon.
>
> That evening REAR Div HQ was ordered to join MAIN Div HQ as there were not sufficient forces to protect both during the hours of darkness.

To improve this situation, 8 Para was eventually ordered to move to positions on the wood edge south-west of Kopenhof. Colonel Hewson recalled:

> The tracks in the wood led in every conceivable direction, darkness was coming on and groups of enemy were becoming quite active and soon it was very obvious that the battalion was utterly and completely lost. The decision was made to stay put where we were and send out patrols. There were a few clashes with the enemy and prisoners were taken. This activity startled Div HQ in no mean way and caused them to 'stand-too' most of the night.'

When dawn broke, as Colonel Hewson said, 'miracle of miracles', 8 Para found its self secure and in the intended place!

Despite the presence of enemy in the woods and fields around Kopenhof the exhausted Headquarters staff spent most of the night in the routine of planning subsequent operations, albeit punctuated by alarms that had them regularly 'standing-too' in their defensive positions, when the firing was a little too close for comfort. The 6th Airborne Division after action report records that:

See map page 125

> *At 2245 hrs Maj Gen MB RIDGEWAY, Commanding XVIII US Corps (Airborne) in company with Maj Gen WM MILEY, Commanding 17 US Airborne Div, visited Div HQ and issued orders for 25 March. His instructions were to maintain the positions then occupied by the Div; for 6 Airlanding Brigade to be relieved by 157 Brigade of 15 (Scottish) Div during the night 25/26 March, and for the Div to be prepared to advance at first light 26 March to secure the phase line 'PARIS'. 17 US Airborne Div was ordered to secure phase line LONDON on 25 March.*

Moving around the Corps area in a Jeep with only a small escort was a not inconsiderable risk. On his way back to his headquarters, co-located with 17th US Airborne's:

> *…the Corps Commander drove into a considerable number of Germans going east from 3 Parachute Brigade area. He was fired on and grazed in the shoulder. It is claimed that he shot at least one German himself. The majority of this party of Germans were rounded up later in the night by 5 Parachute Brigade.*

Senior US commanders were always prepared to be active on the battlefield, preferring face-to-face contact to exchange of lengthy coded messages.

5 Para Brigade

In the more open country covering the Division's northern flank, Brigadier Poett's men spent most of the afternoon digging-in but had to put up with regular fusillades of small arms fire and the occasional mortar bomb. At 1730

Gunners of 53 (Worcester Yeomanry) Airlanding Light Regiment ready to open fire with their 105 mm howitzer.

hours, however, the expected and well organized counter-attack developed from the north across DZ B, which Colonel Pine-Coffin's 7 Para had now abandoned. This was not the heavy armoured attack expected but an attack by 7th *Fallschirmjager* Division, supported by SP guns that closed on 13 Para's position. As an experienced and efficient Division that also benefited from 1st Aiborne Division's lessons at Arnhem, the guns of 4 Airlanding Anti-Tank Battery (8 x 17-Pounder and 8 x 6-Pounder) and battalions' medium machine guns were all sited in pits, albeit incomplete, that gave some protection against enemy fire. To deal with the infantry, the Brigade's medium Vickers machine guns were sited with interlocking and overlapping arcs of fire. Indirect support was immediately available from a battery of 75mm guns of the 53 (Worcester Yeomanry) Airlanding Light Regiment, who were positioned on DZ P in the centre of the Divisional area. Also available west of the Rhine were the 4.2-inch mortars of the Recce Regiment. In the event of a crisis, the Commander Royal Artillery could direct all his divisional assets against a specific target and call for fire from XII Corps, which would bring a massive weight of fire down on Target Groups code named COUSIN, CULPRIT and CLOG that surrounded 5 Para Brigade. The fact that the Brigade was in position, with nearly finished trenches and ready to face an enemy counter-attack, fully justifies General Ridgeway's decision to drop on his objectives. With all this fire available, it is hardly surprising that the enemy counter-attack was broken up before reaching 13 Para's position.

It is recorded that 5 Brigade 'spent a relatively quiet night' and the following day watched battalions of 15th Scottish fighting their way towards them.

Counter-Attacks

6 Airlanding Brigade had secured their three bridges across the Issel and driven-off, killed or captured elements of *Kampfgruppe Karst* that were west of the river and set about digging-in, with battalions having already lost over a third of their landing strength. While the infantry dug, the Royal Engineers prepared the bridges for demolition, should they be in danger of recapture by the enemy.

RAF Sergeant Stan Jarvis was amongst the glider pilots to be deployed to a sector of the Brigade's perimeter, between the two forward infantry battalions, on the banks of the Issel at 1800 hours.

I RUR dug-in on the banks of the Issel.

The German troops were approximately 250 yards away beyond the River Issel, therefore we were instructed to dig slit trenches for protection. It was comparatively quiet until about 8 P.M except for the occasional duel between our Bren guns and the German equivalent, of Spandaus *– then suddenly a vast series of whines were heard overhead followed by crashes, the noise was tremendous. The Second Army had started a bombardment beyond the Autobahn to prevent the enemy bringing up reserves. Incandescent shells ceaselessly passed over for a couple of hours, which was very reassuring as they were from our side! The bombardment suddenly stopped and the silence was almost deafening!*

The German armour, largely neutralised by close air support sorties flown by Allied fighter bombers during daylight, needed to capture the Issel bridges for their own operations but, more importantly, deny their use to the British for their breakout. They now planned to launch an attack under cover of darkness. During the evening of 24 March, 2 Ox and Bucks LI, who had in the last of the daylight completed their defences, reported enemy activity on the approaches to the road bridge just after 2000 hours:

… B Company began to hear movement of tracked vehicles in Ringenburg and the Mediums [artillery] began a series of impressive and encouraging shoots. However, tanks and some infantry approached B Company's [road] bridge and the infantry got into houses just on the other side of the river.

186

Enemy mortaring and artillery fire, which had increased steadily across the Divisional area, engaging opportunity targets, was now concentrated in support of the attack. Lieutenant Denis Edwards of D Company wrote:

> *...my section was sheltering below a high embankment when the enemy began a powerful bombardment of the area. A lot of heavy stuff was crashing in all around the place and, without well-dug trenches such as we had in Normandy, it was impossible to find anywhere that offered good protection.*
>
> *There were several of us crouched in the lee of the embankment when a large shell exploded on the top of the bank just above my head, killing many of those in the immediate area ...I remember nothing else for the next 36 hours.*

Edwards was one of a significant number of airborne soldiers reported Killed in Action during VARSITY, only to have the administrative error later corrected when he was located in the Second Army's medical chain.

Initially the enemy's attacks were driven back and, although 'impressive and encouraging', in darkness, friendly artillery was far less effective and, around midnight, the enemy were able to press home their attack on the Road Bridge. The regimental historian wrote:

> *Our anti-tank guns* [6-pounders] *engaged the enemy and scored hits, but the tanks were too heavy and continued to threaten the bridge. The fighting around the bridge in darkness was very confused. A 'B' Company position on the east of the bridge was overwhelmed, and Lieutenant Clarke led his platoon in a charge to retake it and was subsequently decorated for this action.*

The situation was, however, only temporarily restored and as enemy pressure again built on B Company, Colonel Darrel-Brown, sought permission to blow the bridge if it was likely to be captured. Authority to blow was duly delegated from Brigade HQ to the Ox and Bucks and amidst the fighting the Sapper firing party went forward to insert the detonators into the circuit, thus arming the demolition.

At the same time, HQ 6 Airlanding Brigade made counter-attack plans and issued orders to 12 Devons to be prepared to deploy from Hamminkeln in support of the Oxs and Bucks LI, to either occupy defensive positions vacated by counter-attacking troops or to deliver a counter-attack themselves. In turn, 5 Brigade received a warning order to occupy the Hamminkeln strong point, with 7 Para, should the Devons have to deploy.

At 0200 hours, with the enemy tanks and infantry again advancing from the line of the Autobahn and the 6-pounders able to do little to stop the tanks, it was apparent that the remains of B Company were not going to be able to hold the enemy. According to a Light Infantryman 'one large tank came perilously close. We hoped it was actually on the bridge when the order was given for it to be bridge to be blown'. This attack was shortly after 0230 hours and at 0240, HQ 6 Airlanding Brigade received word that demolition of the small but vital structure was complete.

The Devon's counter-attacks to secure the Oxs and Bucks's positions were not required, as with the blowing of the bridge the enemy armour were unable to cross the river and their supporting infantry fell back under heavy fire. The medium artillery thereafter covered the direct approach to the river with a standing barrage.

The enemy were, however, not content to let the matter rest and directed infantry attacks around the open northern or left flank of the Ox and Bucks. The 6th Airborne report recorded:

> Shortly before dawn small parties of enemy infiltrated into the NORTHERN edge of 2 OXS & BUCKS area and set light to buildings there. In spite of efforts to clear them some enemy remained in that area most of 25 March.

At 0730 hours, 1 RUR reported that two tanks had attempted to rush the bridge but what was probably the leading element of an attack, was halted by a 17-pounder sited to cover the bridge. One tank was knocked out and the other damaged. The enemy infantry decided not to press the point!

With the return of daylight, the Allied airmen were again able to mount close air support and air interdiction patrols. The Airborne report continued:

> During the day a continuous air 'cab-rank' was maintained over the area and a total of about twelve targets were attacked with good results. Tac R [Tactical Air Reconnaissance] later reported only slight movement on the roads leading to the bridgehead.

The Link-up

While contact between patrols had been made west of the Dieserfordterwald the previous afternoon, 15th (Scottish) Division started to arrive in 6th Airborne's positions in strength on the morning of 25 March. The patrol mounted by 7 Para at the gap in the woods code named FORTNUM was approached by 6 KOSB at 0900 hours to the relief of the beleaguered CANLOAN Lieutenant Patterson, whose task of holding a key piece of terrain had, in retrospect, been more fitting for a company than a platoon.

Almost as soon as the amphibious crossing of the Rhine was under way, before dawn on 24 March, the Royal Engineers, with the largest ever accumulation of bridging equipment, started work on their pre-recced ferry and bridging sites. Breaching the massive earthen flood dykes, bringing forward, off-loading and beginning to assemble components were all a part of the first phase of a well-rehearsed and thoroughly planned operation. The first ferries to be established were at the DD tank entry points. One Sapper officer recalled:

> … our Engineering Company was in the front of the assault under a huge barrage of artillery. It was our job to bulldoze the ramps down to the river, drive in the posts to guide the tanks down to where the floating bridges were being assembled and place them into position.

According to the 6th Airborne Division VARSITY report:

> During the night, considerable traffic from the RHINE started to

The 'tail' of the 6th Airborne Divisions vehicles assembles, having crossed the Rhine.

pass through 3 Parachute Brigade area. Visitors to 3 Parachute Brigade HQ included the Commanding Officer of 44 ROYAL TANK REGIMENT (DD Tanks) and the Commanding Officer of 3 SCOTS GUARDS (Tanks).

The officers and men of 6 Guards Tank Brigade, whose tanks were to be amongst the first across the bridges and come under command of XVIII US Airborne Corps, 'felt their responsibility keenly':

It was difficult at the time to forget the tragedy of the previous September when another tank formation of the Brigade of Guards had been given the task of joining up with another airborne force. Would this be a second Arnhem?

The Commanding Officer and squadron leaders of 3rd Tank Battalion, The Scots Guards (3 Tk SG), who were to join 6th Airborne, flew to England to meet officers of the Division during March and officers of the Brigade's other battalions had travelled to France to meet 17th US Airborne to ensure they had a complete and mutual understanding of the plan and to meet those they would be working with. Thus, another failing of MARKET GARDEN was addressed.

On 24 March 3 TK SG joined the Division's radio command net late in the afternoon, as they moved from hide to hide down to the Rhine. Their final hide was near the riverside village of Wardt where they waited until around midnight before being called down to the Class 50/60 rafts. The tanks were carefully loaded onto the rafts one at a time before being towed across the river to undergo the equally difficult operation of off-loading. It took a long time to get even the first tank across and into an assembly area on the east bank.

As soon as the first squadron was complete, the Left Flank Squadron, it drove four miles on narrow country roads across the flood plain. These roads were only designed for light traffic but at 0430 hours on 25 March, the Canadian Para Battalion's war diary recorded the arrival of the first armour in a clearing in the western part of the Diersfordterwald. The Airborne Corps was thus provided with armoured reinforcements little more than sixteen hours after their descent. However, the Churchills were held in the forest under Corps control until the regiment as a whole was assembled some three hours later but with the favourable operational situation they were not called on until the breakout.

This meant that it was not until 1045 hours on the 25th that the forward elements of 6th Airborne Division received the support of 'heavy metal' when '…one squadron of DD Tanks arrived in the area and moved to the vicinity of 6 Airlanding Brigade HQ. One battery of self-propelled anti-tank guns also soon arrived'. The DD tanks of 44 RTR had of course crossed the river the day before and the squadron (minus several tanks KO) was to be used to bolster the forward Divisional reserve, waiting in the woods around LZ P. The Battery of M10 tank destroyers started to arrive, having crossed the river by Class 50/60 ferries, with 6 Airlanding Brigade at 1030 hours. The deployment of a troop M10 to help support the companies holding the Issel bridges convincingly confirmed the balance of combat power in favour of the British Airborne troops.

The vehicles of the Division's Main Land Tail, who had left UK on 15 and 19 March loaded with supplies, were, thanks to a careful convoy schedule, now waiting to cross the Rhine along with sixty-nine preloaded DUKWs. These vehicles only required entrances and exits to the river and could cross on demand with few restrictions, while the Land Tail had to await completion of ferries and bridges and their turn in the order of priority to cross to the east bank. Advanced detachments were the first to cross during the course the 25th, followed by an RASC Light Transport Platoon during the afternoon.

US infantry and armour pressing forward to link up with 17th US Airborne Division.

Breakout

With units of 15th Scottish Division advancing east through the northern edge of 6th Airborne Division's area and both armour and combat supplies coming into the Divisional area, the orders given by General Ridgeway for the breakout could be put into action. During the night of 25 March, 157 Infantry Brigade took over 6 Airlanding Brigade's area, releasing that brigade for the beginning of the breakout to the east.

The fighting west of the Rhine had exhausted the *Wehrmacht* and the descent of an airborne corps in the heart of their position to the east of the river had dislocated their defences. Consequently, progress was swift and by 31 March, according to the Second Army historian:

> *There were east of the River RHINE, under command of Second Army, eight infantry divisions, four armoured divisions, two airborne divisions and four independent armoured brigades. All initial objectives had been gained, the defence line of the enemy had been broken and Second Army was 40 miles on from the river.*
>
> *It was estimated that 30,000 casualties were inflicted on the enemy during these operations while in the period 24-31 March, Second Army incurred losses to the extent of 233 officers and 2,491 other ranks.*

A week after the assault crossing and parachute drop, Field Marshall Montgomery was able to issue his intentions:

> *…To exploit the present situation rapidly, and to drive hard for the line of the River ELBE, so as to gain quick possession of the plains of Northern GERMANY.*
>
> *Second Army will operate strongly to secure the line of the River ELBE between WITTENBERGE and HAMBURG.*

In less than six weeks of the Rhine crossing the war in Europe was over.

CHAPTER ELEVEN

Tours of the VARSITY Battlefields

This tour can be conducted as a study in its own right or as a part of a tour of the wider Rhine crossing battlefields (See *Battleground Operation* PLUNDER). As the first VARSITY stand is just off the main Route 8, the Wesel, Rees, Emmrich road, it is easy to link with the individual TURNSCREW, WIDGEON and TORCHLIGHT (components of PLUNDER) itineraries as required. The tour is designed for light vehicles up to the size of a small mini bus. Width of roads, size of turning points and weight restrictions preclude an unrecced coach tour and even then, the pace of change to local road regulations, as Germany 'greens' itself, makes a recent recce advisable. As I have said elsewhere, the Germans do not have the same slightly cavalier attitude road laws, as fellow Europeans further west! Equally, for the car driver, I have avoided directing visitors down roads signed *'Anliger Fri'* or 'access only', similarly I have avoided apparently easily motorable roads that are now dedicated to cyclists.

To save space and repetition and splitting up the story, these tour instructions are brief. Please refer to the text for details of the action.

General

In common with many of the battlefields of North West Europe, time has changed the patterns of human habitation; villages have expanded and roads built or fallen into disuse. However, unlike the immediate Rhine flood plain, where the unparalleled demand for aggregate to rebuild the nearby Ruhr has left its mark on the battlefield, around the Dieserfordterwald there has been little change. Thanks to the German's traditional farming methods, the country has retained much of its original character, other than the inevitable urban sprawl. Sadly, this is particularly marked around Hamminkeln, which is now a small town rather than a large village, and has spread across LZs O and U to the Issel. Despite these changes, spending half a day plus motoring around this area is thoroughly worthwhile. Those who wish to make use of the network of paths through the Dieserfordterwald, should consult specialist walking maps, as much of the forest is a military training area and rights of way do not necessarily reflect the paths shown on maps.

It is worth avoiding the period late June through to mid late September, as visitors to the VARSITY area during this period find views of battlefields are increasingly obscured by tall maize/corn. It is easier to see and understand the battlefield in autumn and late winter or in the spring.

The VARSITY Tour

The tour starts on the Route 8 Wesel to Rees Road. To reach stand One:

From Wesel, follow the signs to Rees and Emmrich and onto the Route 8. Drive north-west into the forest area. At the Diersfordt cross-roads you will see the green and yellow sign to the Dieserfordter German Cemetery. It is best to visit the cemetery at the end of the tour, so continue over the cross-roads and along the N8. Drive through Bergfurth and pass over the 'New Cross-Roads' (signed Bisslich and Hamminkeln), remaining on Route 8, towards the northern end of the forest. 200 yards after the crossroads, the forest ends and one drives out into open fields. Park in the lay-by by the first buildings on the left, taking care not to obstruct

194

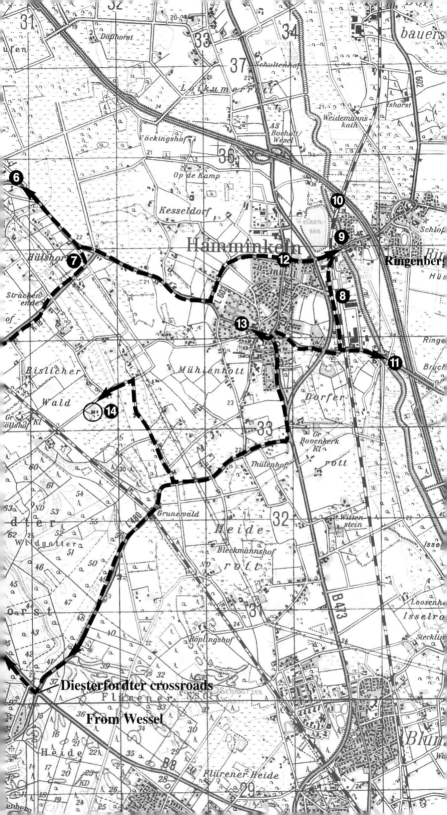

Diesterfordter crossroads

From Wessel

the bus stop or the cycle/footpath. Walk back 100 yard and cross the road to a track that leads across DZ A. This is Stand 1.

If approaching **from Rees**, follow the signs to Wesel, drive through Mehr and past the hamlet of Höfges. Approaching the forest slow and look out for Duisberger Strasse and Alt Poststrasse and park by the buildings. The track to Stand 1 is a further 100 yards towards the wood and across the road. It is advisable not to park in the entrance to the track as it is used with surprising frequency.

Stand 1 – DZ A 3 Para Brigade

Walk north east down the track across DZ A to an extension of the forest (The Axe Handel). To your right, on the forest edge, were the RV's of 1 Canadian Para. On reaching the wood line turn left off the track and follow the broad field margin to the head which is now significantly wider than it was in 1945. The map on page 107 is an excellent aid to orientating ones self to the ground.

Stand 2 – Bergerfurth, 1 Canadian Para's Objective

Return to your car and drive into the wood towards Wesel. Turn left (signed Hamminkeln) at the New Cross-Roads. Turn almost immediately right into Bergfurth (no through road) and park where the tracks radiate in all directions. The road you have just followed the line of a forest track. This is the centre of A Company 1 Canadian Para's defensive area, once the battalion had cleared the hamlet of Bergerfurth.

Stand 3 – Schneppenberg, 9 Para's Objective

The majority of the deserted wood is now a *Bundeswhere* military training area and technically off limits. Those proceeding beyond the barrier on the track that extends from the road you parked on, do so at their own risk.

Walk 200 yards through the wood. Take the left turn and follow the track up hill and then right to the crest of the Schnepenberg feature, which was selected from the map as 9 Para's objective and position from which they would patrol. From this position, the visitor can appreciate 9 Para's advantages; some good observation and the benefit of high ground against counter-attacking

Germans. Their disadvantages; thick undergrowth and some covered approaches for the enemy are equally obvious. In the winter months, depressions in the ground can be clearly seen. It would be nice to think that they were the remains of 9 Para's trenches but the reality is that they are probably the result of far more recent military training.

Stand 4 – Bergfurth and Bridge A

To reach the site of 3 Brigade HQ and 224 Field Ambulance either drive back to the New Crossroads, turn left and park near the yellow painted Landgathaus Bergfurth or take the well made footpath from the parking heading through Bergfurth towards the road. The advantage of this is that the visitor sees the small piece of high ground on the left where a Canadian platoon dug-in. Almost opposite the Gasthaus is a large brick building, which was used by the Field Ambulance, walking towards the cross roads HQ 3 Para Brigade was set up in and around house No 421.

Continue towards the New Crossroads and turn left towards Bislich. Bridge A, now a mere culvert on the modern highway is a short distance down the road, adjacent to the gravel works. Going a little further it is possible to appreciate the country across which 15th Scottish approached in their advance from the Rhine.

Stand 5 – FORTNUM (B2)

Return to the Route 8 and at the New Cross Roads take the road signed towards Hamminkeln. After a thousand yards there is a crossroads (the second left turn) onto a minor road (Harderwycker Weg). Follow the road/track due north to a hamlet around a T-junction and park here. The railway crossing is down the track to the right. This is the area where Lieutenant Patterson fought his mobile action around this key gap in the woods that gave access to 5 Para Brigade's position. This is also the area where the second phase link-up with 15th Scottish Division was made on D+1.

Stand 6 – DZ B 5 Para Brigade

Return to the main road and turn left, crossing the railway line via a modern embankment. At the T-junction, with the tower like, white painted, electricity sub station, turn left towards Mehrhoog. After a thousand yards, the road starts to bend to the left. Slow down and look out for a small turning (Heckenweg) to the right on the crown of the bend. Here it is possible to park safely. DZ B is in the fields to the right of the road. The Brigade's Supply Drop Point (SDP) is to the left of the road.

Stand 7 – 5 Para Brigade Position

Leaving 7 Para to clear the DZ of supplies, wounded and stray men and to temporarily cover approaches to the Divisional area from the north, the remainder of the Brigade moved a thousand yards south-east towards Hamminkeln to dig-in. Drive back towards the White Tower and the junction. Just before entering the 70 KM speed limit around the junction, turn right onto the old road that runs parallel to the modern highway. Park here. This was the centre of 13 Para's defensive position. 12 Para were dug-in on open ground, across the main road to the north-east, towards but short of the autobahn. Traffic on the autobahn can be glimpsed between the trees. 7 Para was eventually withdrawn from DZ B, through 13 Para, into reserve.

Stand 8 – Hamminkeln Station

Continue towards Hamminkeln but do not go into town. Instead, follow the main road to the left onto the town's bypass, signed Ringenberg and 473. At traffic lights/crossroads with the 473 go straight across and turn right just after the Aldi Sud. Follow this road (the railway can be glimpsed between the bushes immediately to the left. Pass the small Hamminkeln station and gasthaus and park on the hard standing. Between this point and the central area of the now sprawling Haminkeln village was LZ O used by the Ox and Bucks LI. Sadly, modern buildings and roads have replaced the stacks of Dieserfordterwald timber awaiting shipment around which the Oxs and Bucks fought in March 1945.

Stand 9 – LZ O1 Road Bridge

Retrace your steps to crossroads and park in or near the Aldi car park. Walk down to the junction; turn right towards Ringenberg, cross the railway line to reach the Road Bridge across the steep banked River Issel. Just to the north (left) is the Railway Bridge (LZ O2). Those visitors expecting to see the Ox and Bucks LI memorial will be disappointed as it was moved when the bridge was replaced and the road widened.

Stand 10 – The Rail Bridge

Having crossed the Road Bridge, take the next left onto a road through some modern housing. Turn left at the T-junction and at the end of the road take the track into the wood. The original rail bridge, captured by B Company 2 Ox and Bucks Light Infantry, is immediately in front of you, complete with bullet holes and strike marks.

Stand 11 LZ X – RUR Bridge

Drive back past Hamminkeln Station, turn left onto the main road and cross the railway line. This is LZ U and the RUR's objective (U1), the Road Bridge, lies beyond. Being less developed, the action in this area is easier to envisage.

Stand 12 – Hamminkeln outskirts 12 Devons

Drive back to the traffic lights/crossroads with the Route 473 and turn right (Bocholt). At the next crossroads turn left off the 473 on to the bypass (Weststrasse) around the north Hamminkeln. Where the main road makes a sharp bend to the right, take the left turn signed Haminkeln, onto Mehrhoogstrasse. This road into the centre of the village was 12 Devon's axis of advance to their objective. The buildings are now more densely packed but the older houses were the ones used as cover by Colonel Gleadell and his small group of airborne soldiers.

Stand 13 – Hamminkeln *Orst Mit* (Village centre)

The village or now a small town has little remaining of wartime vintage that members of 12 Devons would recognize but the churches have been rebuilt and a number of substantial brick buildings remain amidst the modern constructions. At weekends,

Haminkeln makes a good place to stop before completing the tour. There are seven gasthauses or stube to choose from, all serving typically wholesome German food. Midweek visitors, however, will usually have to make do with the Turkish kebab house (open all day), the Chinese restaurant or the inevitable pizzeria.

Stand 14 – LZ P – Kopenhof

From the crossroads at the centre of town, leave Hamminkeln to the south, signed towards Wesel 9 Km, passing on the way out, the new *Rathaus* (town hall), which stands on the site of that used by the Germans as a headquarters. Join the 473 to Wesel and continue south for four hundred yards.Turn right at the next T–junction, signed Bislich. Take the first right turn after the pylon line and follow a minor road (Westfeldweg) north to LZ P. At the T-junction, turn left and stop by the first farm complex on the left (44 Bislicherstrasse). This is Kopenhof (renamed Steffens), the site of Main HQ 6th Airborne Division in the centre of LZ P.

Stand 15 – Diesterfordter German Cemetery

Return to the Hamminkeln – Bislich road and turn right. Drive south-west across the railway line, along the edge of the wood line and into the Diersfordterwald. Cross the main Route 8 (Emmericherstrasse) following the green and yellow *Kriedsgärberstätte* signs to the cemetery.

The cemetery is several hundred yards on the left, on the edge of the village of Diersfordt, in the woods.. The remains of 538 soldiers, most of whom were killed on 24 March, were collected from field graves across the battlefield. However, 109 bodies are 'unknown', which is a high proportion for the North West European Campaign. This perhaps reflects the less careful approach to burial of the enemy taken by an advancing army. The stone crosses are typical of German military cemeteries, with often two names per grave.

In accordance with German practice, other bodies were repatriated to hometowns for burial or were laid to rest in village cemeteries.

This concludes the tour. Return to the R8 and turn left to Rees or right to Wesel.

The Allied Cemeteries

There are several other cemeteries in the area that will be of interest to those studying Operation VARSITY. These are:

Reichswald Forest Cemetery

This cemetery is sited within the Reichswald Forest on the Route X between Kleve in Germany and Gennep in Holland, on the German side of the border. It is the largest CWGC cemetery, in terms of area, and contains 7,654 graves. One hundred and sixty two of the burials are unknown. There are also 79 graves of other nationalities, most of them Poles who fought with the Polish Armoured Division, as a part of the First Canadian Army.

After the War, thousands of graves of soldiers and airmen were concentrated from burial places across western Germany. Most of the soldiers were killed in the Battle of the Rhineland, some dieing fighting in the forest itself in February 1945. A significant number also died during the early stages of Operation PLUNDER, among them are members of the Highland and Scottish Divisions, along with men of 6th British Airborne Division, whose bodies were moved from Hamminkeln. The Army graves are on the right, as one enters the cemetery.

Nearly 4,000 airmen are buried in the cemetery. Some lost their lives in supporting the advance into Germany but the majority died in during the bomber campaign against targets in Germany, and were brought to the Reichswald from cemeteries in the neighbouring area. Graves were concentrated here from cemeteries in Dusseldorf, Krefeld, Monchen-Gladbach, Essen, Cologne, Aachen, Dortmund and many other places in the area. Some were first buried in isolated graves where their aircraft crashed; by a roadside, a riverbank, in a garden or a forest.

Rheinberg War Cemetery

Rheinberg is a small town to the west of the Rhine, three miles from the River and nine miles south of Wesel. The Cemetery is about two miles south-west of the town on the Kamp-Lintfort road. Most of the 3,335 burials were airmen who died in bombing attacks on Germany. Their graves were concentrated here from cemeteries and isolated, wayside graves near where their aircraft crashed; by a roadside, a river bank, in a garden or a forest. From Cologne alone, over 450 Air Force dead who had been buried by the Germans were re-interned here.

There are also over 400 soldiers buried in the cemetery. Many of whom were killed in the Battle of the Rhineland. Operation PLUNDER and the advance to the Elbe. Among them are West Countrymen and Scots who died in the battle for Goch in February 1945 and others who fell in the stubborn fighting for Lingen, which was cleared by the 3rd Division on 6 April.

Order of Battle – Airborne Assault Phase

6th Airborne Division (operational grouping)
Main HQ   Major General Bols
Dets 22 Independent Para Company

3 Parachute Brigade
HQ 3 and Signal Squadron Para Brigade - Brigadier
    Hill
8 Para Battalion
9 Para Battalion
1st Canadian Para Battalion
One troop 3 Airlanding Anti-Tank Battery RA (6-pounder)
In support: Three field regiments RA 52nd Division's Artillery
    Group
Troop 3 Para Squadron RE
224 Para Field Ambulance
Detachment Glider Pilot Regiment

5 Parachute Brigade
HQ and Signal Squadron 5 Para Brigade - Brigadier Poett
7 Para Battalion
12 Para Battalion
13 Para Battalion
4 Airlanding Anti-Tank Battery RA (8x17-pounder, 8x6-
    pounder)
One battery 53 (Worcestershire Yeomanry) Airlanding Light
    Regiment RA (12x75mm)
One medium regiment RA 52nd Division's Artillery Group
Part 591 Para Squadron RE
225 Para Field Ambulance
Detachment Glider Pilot Regiment

6 Airlanding Brigade
HQ and Signal Squadron 6 Airlanding Brigade - Brigadier
    Bellamy
1 Royal Ulster Rifles
2 Ox and Bucks Light Infantry

12 Devons

3 Airlanding Anti-Tank Battery RA less two 6-pounder troops and one 17-pounder section (6x17-pounder)

One battery 53 (Worcestershire Yeomanry) Airlanding Light Regiment RA (12x75mm)

One medium regiments RA 52nd Division's Artillery Group

195 Airlanding Field Ambulance

Divisional Reserve

Two Locust troops 6 Armoured Recce Regiment

One 6-pounder troop and one 17-pounder section from 3 Airlanding Anti-Tank Battery RA

After link up with sea tail:

6 Airlanding Anti-Tank Battery RA (4x17-pounder, 12x6-pounder)

Support

8 Army Group Royal Artillery (general support to XVIII US Airborne Corps) – one field, one medium and one heavy regiments RA, plus 3 battalions of 155mm from Ninth US Army.

Divisional Troops

Detachment Divisional Rear HQ

HQ 53 Worcestershire Yeomanry Regiment RA

Detachments 2 Forward Observation Unit RA

6 Airborne Division Ordnance Field Park

Land Tail (after link up)

Divisional Rear HQ (less detachment)

22 Independent Para Company (less detachment)

6 Armoured Recce Regiment (less two Locust troops and 4.2" mortar troop)

One Squadron 44 RTR (DD Sqn less 17-pounder)

One SP Anti-tank battery

Appendix II

Award of
THE VICTORIA CROSS

B. 39039 Corporal Frederick George Topham

1st Canadian Parachute Battalion

On 24 March 1945, Corporal Topham, a medical orderly, parachuted with his Battalion onto a strongly defended area east of the Rhine. At about 1100 hours, whilst treating casualties sustained

in the drop, a cry for help came from a wounded man in the open. Two medical orderlies from a Field Ambulance went out to this man in succession but both were killed as they knelt beside the casualty. Without hesitation and on his own initiative Corporal Topham went forward through intense fire to replace the orderlies who had been killed before his eyes. As he worked on the wounded man, he was himself shot through the nose. In spite of severe bleeding and intense pain he never faltered in his task. Having completed immediate first aid, he carried the wounded man steadily and slowly back through continuous fire to the shelter of the woods.

During the next two hours Corporal Topham refused all offers of medical help for his own wound. He worked most devotedly throughout this period to bring in wounded, showing complete disregard for the heavy and accurate enemy fire. It was only when all casualties had been cleared that he consented to his own wound being treated. His immediate evacuation was ordered, but he interceded so earnestly on his own behalf that he was eventually allowed to return to duty.

On his way back to his company he came across a carrier, which had received a direct hit. Enemy mortar bombs were still dropping around, the carrier itself was burning fiercely and its own mortar ammunition was exploding, an experienced officer on the spot had warned all not to approach the carrier. Corporal Topham, however, immediately went out alone in spite of the blasting ammunition and enemy fire, and rescued the three occupants of the carrier. He brought these men back across the open and, although one died almost immediately afterwards, he arranged for the evacuation of the other two, who undoubtedly owe their lives to him. This non-commissioned officer showed sustained gallantry of the highest order, for six hours, most of the time in great pain. He performed a series of acts of outstanding bravery and his magnificent and selfless courage inspired all those who witnessed it.

Index